BRONZE THE POWER OF LIFE AND DEATH

Cat. 19

BRONZE

THE POWER OF LIFE AND DEATH

With essays by Martina Droth | Frits Scholten | Michael Cole

Henry Moore Institute, Leeds

Contents

LENDERS TO THE EXHIBITION

Amsterdam, Rijksmuseum
Antwerp, Zeno X Gallery
Cambridge, The Fitzwilliam Museum
Fareham, Royal Armouries Museum of Artillery
Hamburg, Hamburger Kunsthalle
Kassel, Staatliche Museen Kassel, Hessisches Landesmuseum
Leeds Museums & Galleries, Temple Newsam House
London, Victoria and Albert Museum
Munich, Bayerisches Nationalmuseum
Oxford, The Ashmolean Museum of Art and Archaeology
Paris, Musée Carnavalet
Paris, Musée du Louvre
Paris, Musée national du Château de Compiègne
Vienna, Kunsthistorisches Museum

PREFACE

This is the first time the Henry Moore Institute has devoted an exhibition to a single material. Although there are many bronzes in this exhibition about bronze, the subject is, in an important sense, singular rather than plural. This is a show about the meaning of bronze and not a show about the identification or analysis of different bronze casts and editions.

That the subject has moved away from this more familiar terrain to acquire a greater poetic reach is due to the imaginative vision of its curator, Martina Droth. Although our first explorations of the subject were centred on the industrial production of bronze, Martina was soon to be inspired by the close associations of the foundry with the arts of war and of peace – symbolised by the cannon and the bell – and shifted her attention to the meanings carried within the material itself. Thus our exhibition, which ranges from the alchemical to the allegorical, is primarily a suggestive reading of the material as a meaning which overlays, or underlies, the works to which it gives form.

The selection concentrates on the objects and artworks which best embody the associations with parallel worlds: with the elements, with the senses, with the gods, with heaven and hell, life and death. The show should not be read as a survey, or any kind of attempt to provide a *compte-rendu*, but rather as three verses, or chapters, invoking the sense of discovery and excitement which the curator has developed in the course of her research. In this we are fortunate in our guide, for Martina's attention to the details of making has led her towards a closely-observed selection relying at once on a reading of what images the material represents and on what meaning the material itself gives to them.

The protean, shape-shifting, mutable quality of bronze lies behind the whole show, hovering as it does between form and formlessness, and the show ends with contemporary work which characterises the ambiguous way in which bronze offers the promise of extended life at the same time as it takes liveliness away. The poetic direction of this exhibition was enhanced by the early intellectual camaraderie of Frits Scholten of the Rijksmuseum, Amsterdam. Frits' combined strengths of a deep familiarity with the objects of his study, and a belief in the power of exhibitions to represent new ideas in themselves, made him a perfect partner for the Henry Moore Institute in general, and for Martina in particular. We are grateful for the time he was able to devote to our project, in the midst of his, and grateful too to Sabine Conrad who helped Martina to identify and locate potential exhibits for the show.

Research trips made as a result of this preliminary work benefited enormously from the enthusiasm of the curators responsible for their respective collections, and I should like here to mention in particular Sophie Descamps for the Department of Antiquities and Isabelle Leroy-Jay Lemaistre for the Department of Sculpture at the Musée du Louvre, Peta Motture and Greg Irvine from the Victoria and Albert Museum, Claudia Kryza-Gersch at the Kunsthistorisches Museum, Philip Magrath of the Royal Armouries, Julia Poole at the Fitzwilliam Museum and Timothy Wilson of the Ashmolean Museum. (A full list of acknowledgements can be found at the end of the catalogue.)

Martina Droth began working at the Institute in 2002, having recently completed her doctorate on the production and reception of sculpted bronze objects in late nineteenth-century England. This exhibition is the first she has selected, and she has been supported in its development by the team in Leeds, and notably by Stephen Feeke and Gill Armstrong who have, respectively, coordinated the organisation of the show and its catalogue. Essays by Frits Scholten and by Michael Cole, a key author in the field, are supported by an introduction and short texts on the different object groups by Martina Droth. Martina has brought an original eye to an old subject: this catalogue aims to reflect the kind of thinking that has gone into the project and to convey its further possibilities as a subject rich in metaphor and meaning.

Penelope Curtis Curator, Henry Moore Institute

INTRODUCTION

Martina Droth

OBJECTS, as much as the processes that are used to make them, are the outward signs of ideas, and the study of material things allows us to explore the motivations, beliefs and values that underpinned certain productive fields in different times and cultures. The mining and working of metals exemplifies the expression of human thought, and already in the days of Plato the history of the world was divided into metallic ages. Among the earliest bronze objects that we know of are those made not as functional instruments, such as tools or weapons, but as decorative and votive artefacts, suggesting that the development of metallurgic knowledge was not solely driven by survival or dependence.[1] Perhaps more than any other material, bronze demonstrates practical processes to be an extension of creative thought, and indeed prompts us to question how we define efficacy.

As an alloy, bronze manifests an interaction between natural resources and human agencies, and the fashioning of bronze into beautiful or useful things expresses the way that artists, and the cultures of which they were a part, positioned themselves in relation to nature. It is by thinking about how this relationship has been negotiated over time that we can discover some of the intrinsic qualities of materials, and consider how these have defined and enriched the meanings of objects that are fashioned from them.

Bronze and ancient myths

The legendary bronze of Corinth exemplifies the reverence that was once invested in certain copper alloys, and the mystery that still surrounds their beginnings. Pliny, Pausanius, and other ancient sources describe a material so rare and sought-after that blood was shed over it. Its origin, we are told, was the great fire of Corinth in 146 BC, in which all the metals that proliferated in this ancient city ran together and alloyed copper with gold and silver. The legend locates bronze in an enigmatic but unique historical moment, creating a provenance through which the identity of metals could be reconfigured. A metallic hierarchy was established, in which an alloy came to be considered more precious than even pure gold.

Whether these accounts have a factual basis is uncertain; indeed, archaeologists have argued that the material, as far as we understand it, existed long before Corinth was destroyed.[2] But whether fact or fiction, the story gives us a unique insight into the significance and meanings attached to bronze in ancient cultures. Plutarch and Pliny, in their emphasis on the accidental circumstances by which Corinthian bronze was generated, remind us that alloys are products of nature as well as of man, and that fire, essential to human utilisation of metals, is also part of their formation; some of the richest vein deposits are formed when hot magmatic solutions ascend through pressures under the earth.[3] Corinthian bronze is both a gift from nature, and a symbolic reminder of elemental powers that operate beyond cultural control. As fire destroys the city and melts the metallic products of mankind, nature reclaims and purifies her resources, reconstituting them as new matter, more perfect than that which had gone before.[4]

The legend of Corinth suggests that metals were thought of not as inanimate matter, but as responsive and changeable energies. But how are such ideas expressed by objects? The exhibition proposes that, fashioned into images and functional things, bronze drew on experiential effects at different levels. The personification of deities, for example, symbolically referenced supernatural forces, but also hinted at the possibility that such forces might become tangible. Bronze, in its flexibility, warm colour and reflectivity, is unusually suited to the representation of human form and flesh, and statues were often thought of as sentient entities. The melting down of statues, already common in Pliny's time, was not only symbolic, as a sign of victory or regime change, it also rendered the power of the image inactive. For Pliny, the removal of a statue honouring the Roman consul Spurius Cassius, 'who aimed at the kingship' and was executed in 485 BC, signalled that 'even in the matter of a statue they provided against possible ambition'.[5]

Such effects were not confined to large statues. Vessels, like incense burners and oil lamps, perform their function when a substance inside them is heated and made externally visible as they diffuse smoke, light or scent. Their hollow interiors, therefore, represented active and productive spaces that embodied elemental interactions, suggesting that bronze objects were like small theatrical interpretations of the forces of nature. We might describe the chemical reaction taking place in an incense burner as a microcosm of the fire of Corinth itself, or indeed of greater natural phenomena, such as volcanic eruptions or lightning strikes, in which the transformative energy of heat and fire melts or scorches earthly matter. Bronze objects such as those shown in this exhibition can be seen as devices for recreating and making tangible the mysteries of nature and the universe.

Early modern bronze founders

The connections made by early cultures between bronze, nature and the gods, were rediscovered in the Renaissance and revitalised through the collecting and imitating of ancient objects, as a number of works in the exhibition illustrate. In their sophistication, Greek and Roman artefacts were seen as traces of an exemplary and spiritually elevated culture. While this was expressed through a deliberate and self-conscious intellectualising of ancient thought, the desire to emulate ancient production also alludes to an identification with spiritual beliefs. Artistic practices, including the casting of bronze, continued to provide a channel through which artists articulated a reverential regard for nature.

One of the earliest known printed works covering the whole field of metallurgy was written by a Sienese armourer and munitions-maker, Vannoccio Biringuccio. Dating to 1540, *De la Pirotechnia* is valuable not only as a record of the practical approaches that informed all aspects of metalwork, from prospecting and mining to smelting and casting, but for what it reveals about ideas concerning the origins of metals, their development and behaviour. Biringuccio presents metals as organic gifts from nature. He likens the scarcity of copper mines in Italy to the conduct of a farmer who left ripe fruit to 'rot and waste in the fields'.[6] His advocacy of greater exploitation of mineral resources has been described as financially driven and reflective of an 'established capitalistic economy', and indeed, the *Pirotechnia* was unusual for its practical treatment of a field that, in the sixteenth century, was regarded with superstition and closely associated with what Biringuccio labelled the pseudo-science of alchemy.[7]

But Biringuccio's disagreement with the alchemists, as much as his advocacy of mineral exploitation, centres on a particular attitude towards nature that cannot be straightforwardly interpreted as cupidity. While his text in some respects demystifies the field of metallurgy, it nonetheless presents metals as enigmatic manifestations of nature; scientific knowledge, he implies, can provide a tool for managing our relationship with materials, but cannot entirely control them. Bronze, in this context, through its transformation into artefacts, is symptomatic of man's engagement with nature.

An insight into how this engagement was negotiated in the sixteenth century is provided by Benvenuto Cellini's famous narrative about the casting of his 'Perseus' (see Fig. 2 in Frits

Scholten's essay, p. 23).[8] While Cellini's imaginative and exciting tale seems almost antithetical to Biringuccio's rational tone, he draws on parables that, although fantastical, hint at shared ideas about the interaction of elements. The nature of bronze is described as volatile and capricious, and to attempt to cast it is to engage in a process that, while manageable to an extent, is nonetheless dangerous and unpredictable. When, mid-way through melting the metals, Cellini finds the bronze threatening to curdle, he throws all his household pewter into the crucible, implying that it was not possible to know the exact requirements of the material in advance. His cast is subject to the incalculable contingencies of nature: the dryness of the wood, the degree of heat it yields, the unexpected interference of wind and rain that cools the furnace – factors he could anticipate, but not regulate.

While the story of the 'Perseus' cast forms part of the myth-making that characterises the whole autobiography, it also specifically suggests that the demiurgic powers of bronze recognised by the ancients were still palpable to artists in the sixteenth century. Bronze was unquantifiable, and obeyed natural, not human laws. Far from being thought of as inert, metals challenged their users to adapt to nature's bidding. The possibility of accidental and unforeseen outcomes meant that a successful bronze cast not only evinced the founder's technical knowledge, but his intimate connection and empathy with nature's ways. As Frits Scholten and Michael Cole further explain, Cellini not only presents himself as an embodiment of Vulcan, he identifies materially with his statue as an extension of himself: the resurrection of the metal from the brink of disaster coincides with the artist's recovery from a deadly fever; the casting being completed only when he takes charge of the rain and wind sweeping through his workshop; and the single flaw in the cast, the incomplete foot which he had predicted, alludes to the lame leg of the god of the forge.[9] By thus identifying himself bodily with bronze and its determining factors, Cellini suggests that the very act of engaging with materials implicated one in the cycles of nature.

Bronze in the industrial age

The Industrial Revolution initiated a fundamental change in perceptions of materials, and brought about what could be seen as a demystification of metals. Although bronze remained materially unchanged, the way that metals were studied and thought about was no longer rooted in mystical belief. The theological underpinning of a text like the *Pirotechnia* was superseded by a more secularised conception of science; similarly, the elemental danger and volatility that characterised bronze casting in the Renaissance, although by no means eradicated, were by the mid-1800s largely redefined as the collateral risks of manufacturing. Foundry methods became increasingly systematic, and as the processes of bronze-work were rationalised into a sequence of logical steps, the secrecy that had previously surrounded them, and in particular their association

Fig. 1 Aimé Jules Dalou (1838–1902),
'The Triumph of the Republic', 1879–99,
Place de la Nation, Paris

with alchemy, was often ridiculed as an irrational and superstitious misconception of how the world was structured.[10]

While these developments may have stripped bronze of much of its demiurgic associations, it by no means lost its distinct significance as a material; indeed, as the properties of metals and their usefulness became better understood (notably, the conductivity of copper and the creation of electrical energy), opportunities arose to explore the role of bronze anew and redefine it against the background of modern ideas. The vastly diverse and multifaceted impacts of the industrial age make these interpretations difficult to summarise, but one important common denominator was the investment of bronze with specific political meanings, and the recognition that its symbolic associations could be adapted to changing social contexts.

Bronze provided an index for the economic and artistic aspirations of a nation, a development epitomised by the growth of large, independent art foundries in Paris, which turned the reproduction of bronze statuettes into substantial international businesses.[11] The relationship between artists and producers became formalised, creating a new distinction between the professions; in the case of a manufacturer like Barbedienne, this meant that the work which took place in the artist's studio was entirely separated from the end-product made in the foundry. The polished, chiselled surfaces and colorations of a work like François Rude's 'Mercure rattachant ses talonnières' (Cat. 30), a Barbedienne edition, typifies the aesthetic that directly emerged from the newly streamlined bronze industries.[12]

Alongside such private commercial enterprise, bronze founders also played an important civic role, especially in Third Republic France where there was a demand for monuments to mark the emergence of democratic government. The huge human effort invested into, for example, Jules Dalou's colossal monument of the 'Triumph of the Republic' (1879–99, Place de la Nation, Paris) set into a public arena not only an impressive and deeply symbolic bronze sculpture, but brought to attention the foundry-workers who, over some twenty years, cooperatively contributed their particular skills, as well as their labour and energy, to honouring the establishment of democracy (Fig. 1). The symbolism of the monument is clear: Liberty moves forward triumphantly, as her chariot, pulled by lions, crushes a crown and sceptre underneath. She is flanked by workmen who, by their apparel, remind us of the bronze founders involved in creating the monument and who, by extension, symbolically suggest the founders of democracy. The aesthetic of the monument is deliberately baroque, the style Dalou loved most, but which characterised the gilt excesses of the monarchy under the Sun King; recontextualised in the new republic as a national style, Dalou, in his own words, 'put at the service of democracy all the glittering pomp of the century of Louis XIV'.[13]

At a material level, bronze in nineteenth-century France, as much as in ancient Rome and sixteenth-century Italy, was itself an emblem of triumph. The destruction of statues, for example, that we know from Pliny and other ancient sources, continued to be practised across millennia

Fig. 2 Workers remove a statue of
the late Spanish dictator Franco from
San Juan de la Cruz Square, Madrid,
17 March 2005

and into the nineteenth and twentieth centuries. Even if such acts were no longer provoked by auratic impulses, the importance of bronze statues as public statements of power and its loss was undiminished. As Michael Cole's essay in this volume describes, warfare created a need for cannon, and victory brought fresh supplies of bronze, identifying peace as an extension of war which bronze makes manifest. Bronze thus becomes a vehicle for expressing power, not only symbolically, through sculpture, but materially, through the very processes that govern it. Although cycles of destruction and regeneration have specific localised connotations, they also speak of a cycle that is universal and perpetual. Bronze is transformed by heat in the nation's foundries, and the melting down of enemy cannon can be likened to a cleansing by fire; the forms of war are lost, and the material is returned to its neutral state, allowing the nation to reclaim it as a precious resource, to be refashioned into new emblems appropriate to the age.

Conceptualising the meanings of bronze

We perhaps too often assume that the secularisation of science and metallurgy in the industrial age led to an erosion of the resonance and meaningfulness of materials. Undoubtedly, the nineteenth century was shadowed by deeply-felt fears about the negative ramifications of mechanisation, most clearly demonstrated by the apocalyptic thinking of the Arts and Crafts Movement. But these anxieties about the future, which must be seen separately from actual outcomes, tell us very little about how interpretations of materials were affected by the realities of their contemporary employment.[14] The continuing relevance of bronze depended on the adaptation of its unique symbolic resonance to the evolving political landscape.

An important change brought about by the secularisation of metals was that emphasis shifted away from the functional and symbolic interiority of bronze objects (the ancient incense burner with its active interior) and turned towards external forms as a means of diffusing understandable political messages, vividly embodied in the twentieth century by monuments of the communist era and of dictatorships. The striking spectacle of colossal statues of Lenin or Franco, or more recently Saddam Hussein, being brought down, points to the transience of the meanings they represented, and highlights the inevitability that any such overt ideological statement will at some point become subject to change (Fig. 2). Bronze statues have always been recycled, and in a sense this reflects the genesis of the material itself. Bronze is the fleeting witness of world changes over millennia; it can be melted down and reused, but is itself the prehistoric product of nature that, materially, can never be made new. Within radically changing systems and contexts, bronze provides a certain constant, which is irrevocable and which becomes all the more powerful for its embodiment of intransience.

As the closing room of the exhibition seeks to demonstrate, the material significance of bronze, although now explored on more introspective, conceptualised levels, especially in sculptures not conceived for public programmes, still draws on certain truths informed by the origins of materials. Bronze itself is neutral, but the ways in which it is used can provide a conceptual index of the past and the inevitability of change; a channel through which to explore ourselves, how we process, store or obliterate memory, and how we relate to the world around us and to nature. Bronze is a mirror of its context.

NOTES

My special thanks to Nicholas Mead and Penelope Curtis for the encouragement and thoughtful insights they offered me throughout the writing of this catalogue. I am also grateful for the assistance of Ronald Brashear and Kirsten van der Veen at the Dibner Library of the History of Science and Technology, Smithsonian Institution Libraries, Washington, DC, where I was a Baird Society Resident Scholar in June–July 2005.

Abridged references indicated in the notes to the essays are cited in full in the bibliography on p. 112ff.

1   See Robert Maddin, ed., *The beginnings of the use of metals and alloys*, Cambridge, Mass., 1988.

2   See Craddock and Giumlia-Mair, *Corinthium Aes*.

3   John F. Healy, *Mining and metallurgy in the Greek and Roman world*, London, 1978, p. 23.

4   Although the natural association of copper and tin ore in the same matrix is rare, its known occurrence has been cited as an explanation for the discovery of bronze. For a discussion see Forbes, *Metallurgy*, pp. 248–50.

5   Pliny, *Natural history*, p. 27. Carol Mattusch discusses the treatment of statues as 'sensate individuals', including the 'sentencing' of a bronze statue to murder, in her chapter 'The preferred medium: the many lives of classical bronzes', in *The fire of Hephaistos*.

6   Biringuccio, *Pirotechnia*, p. 52.

7   Biringuccio, *Pirotechnia*, translator's preface, p. xiv.

8   Cellini, *Life of Benvenuto Cellini*.

9   The interplay between the material of the statue, Cellini's persona, and the myth of Perseus (who killed Medusa with the aid of a polished bronze shield), are explored in depth in the second chapter of Cole, *Cellini*. See also *The fire of Hephaistos*.

10   There are any number of references to this in metallurgical texts. For an example specifically related to the casting of bronze statues see John Holland, *Memorials of Sir Francis Chantrey, RA, sculptor*, London, 1851.

11   The international expositions that took place throughout the mid-nineteenth century and beyond created a newly competitive international stage on which countries compared their manufacturing skills, and nations took great pride in how they were represented. For a discussion see for example Whitney Walton, *France at the Crystal Palace: bourgeois taste and artisan manufacture in the nineteenth century*, Berkeley, Los Angeles and Oxford, 1992.

12   For more on the Parisian founders see Catherine Chevillot, 'Les stands industriels d'èdition de sculptures à l'Exposition Universelle de 1889: l'example de Barbedienne', *Revue de l'art*, vol. 95, no. 1, 1992, pp. 61–7; and Jacques de Caso's essay on 'Serial sculpture in nineteenth-century France', in *Metamorphoses in nineteenth century sculpture* (exhibition catalogue), ed. Jeanne L. Wasserman, Fogg Art Museum, Cambridge, Mass., 1975.

13   From an obituary notice, 1902, cited by John M. Hunisak, *The sculptor Jules Dalou: studies in his style and imagery*, New York, 1977.

14   Arts and crafts ethics are often interpreted as unilaterally influential, perhaps overstating their actual impact on the wider artistic milieu. For a discussion see my 'The ethics of making: craft and English sculptural aesthetics c.1851–1900', *Journal of Design History*, vol. 17, no. 3, September 2004.

BRONZE, THE MYTHOLOGY OF A METAL

Frits Scholten

IN 'THE BELL', the last episode in *Andrei Rublev*, Tarkovsky's 1966 cinematic masterpiece, Boriska, the son of the deceased bell-maker Nikolka, accepts with youthful hubris the grand duke's commission to cast a huge bell. After Nikolka's death there is no one capable of fulfilling this ambitious commission successfully, but Boriska claims that he has learnt the secret of casting bells from his father. An enormous field furnace is built and a large casting pit dug; together with his helpers, Boriska makes a large clay model of the bell, packed in its mantle. Ignoring the warnings of his assistants, who insist the wall of the mantle is still too thin and will crack during casting, Boriska decides to set his helpers to work, while he himself rests. Feverish activity continues around him: the fires in the furnaces are being stoked to melt the bronze and bring it to the right temperature for casting. The boy, awake again but stupefied by the intoxication of his own audacity, orders his helpers to throw more silver into the furnaces to make the composition of the bronze as good as it can possibly be. Finally, he gives his assistants the signal to start casting, and calls on God's help. The liquid metal flows to the casting pit through numerous channels and

Detail: Fig. 2 Benvenuto Cellini, 'Perseus'

runs into the mould. The next day, after it has cooled, the mantle is cut away and a magnificent bell emerges (Fig. 1). It seems that a miracle has occurred, particularly when Boriska confesses that his father took his secret of bell-casting with him to his grave. 'The Bell' is an extraordinarily accurate account of the casting process, but it is above all a superb metaphor of the artistic, almost divine creative urge with which the true artist makes his ultimate work of art.

The striking parallels between 'The Bell' and one of the most famous passages in Renaissance literature, Benvenuto Cellini's sensational account of the casting of his bronze 'Perseus' (Fig. 2), suggest that Tarkovsky knew this story. Here, too, the artist seems to have been overcome by hubris for, like Boris, Cellini was not at that time an experienced bronze caster.[1] Although as a goldsmith Cellini was familiar with casting small sculptures and objects in precious metals, a monumental bronze statue represented a very different challenge, which led Cellini into the foreign territory of another trade with its own rules, tricks and workshop secrets: that of the professional bronze casters.[2] Cellini, like Boris exhausted from the stress and desperately ill with a fever, left his workshop at the height of the process to rest, leaving the work to his helpers, 'bronze founders, craftsmen, peasants and my own workshop assistants'. When the melting of the bronze began to go wrong, Cellini was forced to rise from his supposed deathbed and take control:

> At this crisis, when the whole gang saw the cake was on the point of melting, they did my bidding, each fellow working with the strength of three. I then ordered half a pig of pewter to be brought, which weighed about sixty pounds, and flung it into the middle of the cake inside the furnace. By this means, and by piling on wood and stirring now with pokers and now with iron rods, the curdled mass rapidly began to liquefy. Then, knowing I had brought the dead to life again [...] I felt such vigour fill my veins that all those pains of fever, all those fears of death, were quite forgotten.[3]

OPPOSITE
Fig. 1 Still from *Andrei Rublev* (Andrei Tarkovsky, USSR, 1966)

Fig. 2 Benvenuto Cellini (1500–71), 'Perseus', 1545–54, Loggia dei Lanzi, Florence

As Michael Cole has convincingly shown, this passage plays an ingenious metaphorical game with animation or, more precisely, reanimation.[4] As the bronze melted and came 'to life again', the sculptor found his own powers restored, as if he too had risen from the dead; and after he succeeded in turning the tide, and the bronze started to flow into the mould, he cried out: 'Oh God! Thou that by Thy immeasurable power didst rise from the dead, and in Thy glory didst ascend to heaven!'[5] Resurrection from death occurs precisely at the culmination of the casting process as the channels fill with the molten bronze. Significantly, Cellini's metaphor of animation relates not only to the statue – a universally familiar *topos* in art literature since Antiquity, which refers both to Ovid's archetypal sculptor Pygmalion and to God's creation of Adam from clay[6] – but also to the metal, to the bronze itself. The mythical notion that bronze is a dead material that can be returned to life should therefore not simply be understood as a metaphor per se: Cellini's words conceal a widely-held belief in the exceptional, vital properties of bronze.

Sixteenth-century metallurgical treatises offer abundant indications that the stages of the process of mining and casting metal were sexualised and personified.[7] Underlying this was the belief that ores grew in the earth under the influence of the stars, that mines and quarries were wombs and that ores were embryos.[8] The engraving *Cathena Aurea Platonis* (The golden chain of Plato) published by Crispijn de Passe the Elder around 1575 (Fig. 3), clearly illustrates how in the sixteenth century this Platonic cosmological system was viewed: God, the angels and the four elements are the main links of the oval chain, while in the lower regions, man, the animals, the plants and finally, in the large pendant below, stone and metal, are attached to the chain with cross-links; around them, in a higher sphere, float the seven planets. They influence the lives of man, animals, plants, stone and metal, but man is also able to influence the world around him. In his influential treatise *De la Pirotechnia* (1540), Biringuccio compared the veins of ore with the veins of living animals and the root systems of trees; gradually, he said, these veins grew upwards, eventually to emerge on the surface, chiefly in the mountains.[9]

Echoes of this organic symbolism can still be heard in modern western languages, for example in the use of the word *materi*al for primal matter, and the word *matrix*, which means womb, as a name for a casting mould. Such sexual metaphors, legends or articles of faith were widespread and not confined exclusively to metallurgy, as Mircea Eliade demonstrated. They rest on complex connotations related to *Terra Mater* symbolism, the roots of which go back to antiquity; implicit in this superstition is the notion that everything which comes from the earth's womb – spring-water, clay, lava, ore – is alive, albeit in a premature state (to speak in terms of pregnancy). In the *Bergbüchlein* of 1500, the earliest known printed metallurgical treatise in the German language, the secret of the genesis of ore is similarly revealed, but here alchemy also plays a part.[10] All metals come from the union of mercury and sulphur, which are female and male, growing under a strict cosmological regime. Gold grows thanks to the power of the sun, silver is influenced by the moon, copper by Venus, tin by Jupiter, lead by Saturn and iron

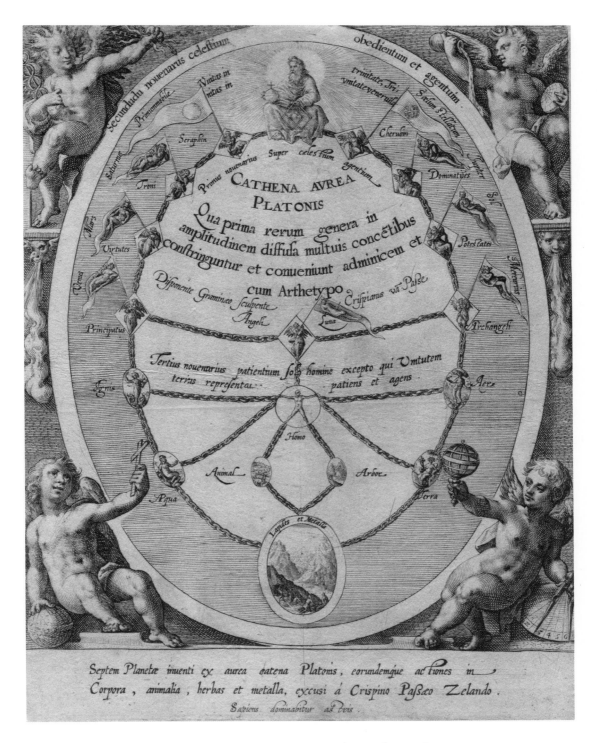

Fig. 3 Title page from *Cathena Aurea Platonis* (The golden chain of Plato), *c.*1575, published by Crispijn de Passe the Elder

by Mars.[11] Popular belief and cosmology come together here with the 'sexual' union of the substances in alchemy.

The same symbolism continued in metallurgy and bronze casting, where the bronze founder assumed the task of Mother Earth, as it were, bringing the premature ores to full term by heating, smelting and refining.[12] The crucible was also described in metallurgy as the *matrix* or womb, and the role of the bronze founder in this whole process is comparable to that of the alchemist. Like the alchemist, he purified crude ores, but in a sense he transmuted them too, by combining them in the right proportions and making them liquid, or animating them to result in a new metal, created by human hands: bronze. By creating new forms from this enlivened material, the bronze founder could align himself with nature and imagine himself as a sort of Creator.[13] Sixteenth-century casting terminology, which was derived from human anatomy, underlined this belief: the flames that heated the crucible, which, as we saw, represented a kind of womb, were fanned with bellows, a symbol of breathing in the force of life, while the 'living', molten bronze was shaped inside the mould, itself thought of as the *matrix* (or womb).[14] In the mould, which was kept together by a metal skeleton or *ossatura*, was the model made of clay and wax, called *anima* or soul. Thus the sculptor built up his image by analogy with God, who created humans from clay and breathed life into them; *fusione* (casting) and *infusione* (animating, inspiring) followed on from one another.[15]

Similar invocations of nature can be seen in the objects themselves, for example in the many life casts that have been made since the sixteenth century, where real animals or plants were enclosed in a mould and then cast. The bronze, or possibly some other medium that can be cast, takes the place of the animal's body and forms a perfect replica. The casting of reptiles or amphibians became so common that this method came to be known as the 'lost lizard' process, a variant on the *cire perdue* or lost wax technique.[16] Bronze lizards, snakes, toads, insects and other lower life-forms were made as statuettes in their own right and as decorative motifs on bronze objects like mortars (Fig. 4). Here the bronze caster played with the notion of having bent nature to his will and even surpassed it: the animals were, so to speak, petrified in bronze, seemingly lifeless, but in fact 'slumbering' in their new guise. Through this form of metamorphosis he encroached on the domain of alchemy, which also sought to create new life in the form of the *homunculus*.[17] Bronze sculptors' preference for the lower animals is probably connected to the special properties that these species were believed to possess. Frogs and toads, for instance, were thought to be born spontaneously, without parents, and Aaron and the Pharaoh's magicians in Moses' Egypt summoned up frogs and insects *ex nihilo* and changed their staffs into snakes.[18] Such examples of magical transformations and metamorphoses in nature provided the mysterious context within which the life casts that the bronze casters and sculptors made had to be understood.

Sculptors also demonstrated the notion of divine creative power in a very different way, by invoking the image of Vulcan, the classical god of the arts of fire. Cellini, for example, told his

Fig. 4 'Lucertole in lotta' (Fighting
Lizards), bronze, 16th century,
collection of Ignazio Vok, Padova

27

patron Cosimo de'Medici that the right foot of his 'Perseus' would not emerge complete from the mould after casting unless he built a much larger furnace, a reference to Vulcan, who, according to Homer, was born with a crippled foot and crooked toes.[19] Similarly, in Adriaen de Vries' relief 'Vulcan's Forge' of 1611, the sculptor identified himself with the smith to the gods (Fig. 5). An almost hidden detail in the back wall of the forge is a personification of *Fama* (Fame), which can be read as a reference to de Vries' own artistry; it is a form of personal artistic praise that is explicitly reinforced by the sculptor's signature, placed prominently on Vulcan's anvil.[20] The smith and his tools, familiar metaphors for the natural process of creation since the Middle Ages, were ascribed with magical and religious powers in Western as well as non-European cultures.[21] In the thirteenth-century *Roman de la Rose* by Jean de Meun, Mother Nature uses a hammer and anvil to bring forth individuals, while at the end of his *Pirotechnia*, Biringuccio presents Cupid as the smith of the fire of love.[22] The popularity of images of Vulcan in art since the sixteenth century probably has to be viewed in the same light, that is to say against the background of his status as the embodiment of divine artistic and skilled creative power.[23]

Sixteenth-century bronze sculptors, as *alter* Vulcans, already enjoyed considerable respect because of the extensive and mysterious technical and artistic skills they had to possess, and they could command extra prestige by casting their statues *aus einem Guss* (in one pour). Being riskier, and technically more complex, this process, which Cellini used for his 'Perseus', demonstrated immense daring and bravura, comparable to carving a complicated composition from a single block of stone.[24] Although it was certainly not essential to cast a statue without any seams, as it was for bells and firearms, the *difficultà* of such an operation, particularly for a complex, open composition like that of the 'Perseus', must have weighed very heavily with Cellini. In this, most probably, a contest with Michelangelo's 'David', which was carved from a single block of marble, played an important role. The challenge lay in the significant chance that the casting would fail, something that Biringuccio had already warned against. This did not, however, deter Giambologna from casting the larger than life-sized horse for the equestrian statue of Cosimo in one pour, in the presence of Don Giovanni de'Medici, in 1592.[25]

Bronze founders faced other technical challenges, including the demand that their statues must have evenly thin walls. To Vasari, it was a mark of quality if the wall of a bronze was as thin as 'una costola di coltello' (the back of a knife), and Florentines in the sixteenth century believed they had surpassed the bronze art of the ancients in the thinness of the walls of their casts.[26] Economical considerations certainly were a factor; a thick wall was a waste of expensive material and a sign of the incompetence of the sculptor. The contract drawn up when Adriaen de Vries went to work for the sculptor Pompeo Leoni in 1586 actually explicitly stipulated: 'and this he must make with the clay core and cover it uniformly with a thin layer of wax on each part'.[27]

The finishing of bronzes was also a matter of professional jealousy. Cellini, after casting the bronze bust of Cosimo de'Medici as a practice-run before making his 'Perseus', wrote:

Fig. 5 Adriaen de Vries (1545–1626),
'Vulcan's Forge', 1611, Bayerisches
Nationalmuseum, Munich

The first cast I took in my furnace succeeded in the superlative degree, and was so clean that my friends thought I should not need to retouch it. It is true that certain Germans and Frenchmen, who vaunt the possession of marvellous secrets, pretend that they can cast bronzes without retouching them; but this is really nonsense, because the bronze, when it has first been cast, ought to be worked over and beaten in with hammers and chisels, according to the manner of the ancients and also of the moderns.[28]

While Cellini hereby consigns the possibility of casting a bronze without having to retouch it to the realm of fable – a self-evident reaction for a goldsmith who was used to chasing metal – his account also betrays unmistakable admiration for this technical feat. In the light of the considerable detail on Cosimo's bust, Cellini's claim that the statue needed virtually no re-touching is particularly remarkable, and typical of his self-aggrandisement. In 1569 one of his contemporaries, Guglielmo della Porta, sent a rough, unworked bronze crucifix to Emperor Maximilian II. This piece, taken straight from the mould, was intended among other things to convince the emperor of the quality of della Porta's *disegno*, and probably also as a demonstration of the high standard of casting.[29] His crucifix has not survived, but there are other sixteenth- and seventeenth-century bronzes that were left unfinished, probably with the same objective in mind. Some of them were experimental castings, like the famous Madonna after a model by Hans Leinberger, which was probably made in connection with work for the large tomb for Emperor Maximilian I in Innsbruck, and a small statue of John the Baptist by the same hand.[30] Such bronze *bozzetti*, or sculptors' sketch models, contributed to the uniqueness of a work, a notion of course not unimportant with a medium like bronze, which was ideally suited to reproduction.

The fascination with *il segreto di gettar le cose* (the secret of casting things) was rife among patrons in the sixteenth and seventeenth centuries and has to be seen against the background of a wide-ranging interest in science, alchemy and technology at the ruling courts of Europe. They were particularly impressed by the complexity of the casting process and this was directly reflected in the high status that founders and sculptors enjoyed in court circles. Cosimo de'Medici, for example, was greatly interested in the mining of ore and in the practical applications of alchemy; his discussions with Cellini about bronze casting, and Benedetto Varchi's catalogue of praise of him, confirm the duke's knowledge and study of metals.[31] As we have already seen, Don Giovanni de'Medici watched Giambologna casting Cosimo's equestrian statue, and the famous equestrian statue for Louis XIV begun by Desjardins is part of the same tradition (Fig. 6); that Adriaen de Vries deliberately left remnants of the runners and vents visible in several of his bronzes can similarly be seen as a demonstration of the complexity of the casting process.

In a period when the technology of casting sculptures was little developed anywhere outside Italy, there was a huge demand for bronze sculptors in Northern Europe. Around 1570 the

Fig. 6 Martin Desjardins (1637–94),
'Louis XIV on Horseback', c.1688–91,
Statens Museum for Kunst, Copenhagen

Holy Roman Emperor, the Habsburg Maximilian II, went to great lengths to secure the services of an Italian-trained sculptor, the *fiammingo* Johan Gregor van der Schardt, who was eventually persuaded to leave Venice for Nuremberg.[32] The situation repeated under Emperor Rudolf II, who made determined efforts to establish a modern bronze foundry at the court in Prague and, more importantly, to attract a skilled caster and good sculptor. He succeeded in his endeavours, although only after failing to lure Giambologna from Florence to Prague: in 1602 Martin Hilliger, a member of a prominent Saxon family of bronze casters, was appointed to set the business to rights at Prague Castle, while de Vries had already been appointed *Kammerbildhauer* a year earlier.[33] Rudolf was driven by an intense desire to compete with the Italian courts, particularly that of Florence, and to outdo his brother Archduke Maximilian III of Tyrol, who had engaged the services of the bronze sculptor Hubert Gerhard – a fellow-countryman of de Vries. The way that sculptors were deployed in the artistic competition between the courts is illustrated by a comment Rudolf made in 1602, when two bronze statues by Gerhard arrived in Prague, as a gift from his younger brother: 'The workmanship is very subtle and clean, only the composition of the same is rather poor, Master Adrian as His Majesty's bronze caster will make the same a great deal better'.[34] His comment led directly to the creation of Adriaen de Vries' group of 'Hercules, Nessus and Deianeira' (Musée du Louvre, Paris), with which the imperial sculptor had to prove to Rudolf that he could indeed make a better composition.

An explanation for the Habsburgs' particular interest in bronze can be found in the medieval notion of the metal as a symbol of strength and durability. This symbolism fuelled a tradition, both north and south of the Alps, of executing major bronze monuments as echoes of classical antiquity. The most prominent Roman statues known during the Middle Ages were, after all, made of bronze and the fact that they had survived since the fall of the Roman Empire was testimony to the durability of the material.[35] But the symbolism of power and durability also had its reverse side: already in antiquity, captured bronze weapons were melted down and the metal reused to cast symbols of glory and peace.[36] A statue made *ex aere capto* was first and foremost, of course, a sign of triumph, but the melting down of enemy bronze could also be an act of exorcism, intended to break the enemy's enchantment of the material, indicating that the metal had been seen as actively apotropaic. Since Antiquity, bronze was seen as an effective means of warding off evil influences. Bronze personifications of the provinces of the Roman Empire were set up on the Capitol in Rome, where, so early medieval legends had it, they warned the Romans of uprisings in the empire, and the equestrian statue of Marcus Aurelius was credited with the power of weakening an enemy army; the city of Naples claimed that a bronze archer, aiming his arrows at Vesuvius, protected the city against eruptions from the volcano; a bronze fly was believed to keep the Neapolitans free of plagues of flies.[37]

The apotropaic quality of bronze was also associated with its ability to produce fine sounds. It rang out throughout the Christian Middle Ages in the innumerable church bells, which were seen as important instruments for warding off the devil and evil spirits. This often led to the individualisation or even personification of the bell as a magically living being, expressed not only in the *sonans,* the ability to make sound, but also in the widespread custom of giving bells (like cannon) names.[38] The earliest record of this goes back to Carolingian times: Alcuinus, the rector of the court school in Aix-la-Chapelle, advocated giving bells a forename, just as living people are given a name.[39] The inscriptions on church bells – as well as on mortars and cannon – are often couched in the first person singular, suggesting that it is the bell itself that speaks: MAGISTER IERADVS DE LEODIO ME FECIT ANNO DOMINI MCCCXVI ORIDA VOCOR (Master Gerardus of Liège made me in the year of our Lord 1316; I am called the Terrible) says the inscription on the bell from the Church of Our Lady in Antwerp.[40] The bell owes its name 'Orida' (Terrible) to its function as an alarm, ringing out to warn of danger and disaster.

Bronze, because it is a man-made metal, was proof *par excellence* of mankind's power to control nature, and consequently the discovery of the metal is anchored in the mythologies of many ancient civilisations. Pliny, for example, believed that bronze casting was originally the exclusive domain of the gods.[41] Casting the crude material in a mould was equated with the genesis of the world out of chaos and the creation of man from clay. Such myths derive from the

Fig. 7 Mimmo Paladino (b. 1948), 'Elmo' (Helmet), 1998, Musée national d'art moderne – Centre Georges Pompidou, Paris

significance that the metal must have had in the Bronze Age, a period that Ovid described as the time when man discovered his ability to defend himself. In the transition from the Stone Age to the Iron Age, man made the revolutionary discovery of smelting and casting a mixture of copper and tin to produce a material that was ideal for the manufacture of weapons, tools and jewellery. Recent archaeological research has demonstrated that these early bronze objects had an important sacred and ritual significance.[42] Many bronze artefacts, particularly axes, were apparently left intentionally in the ground, suggesting a form of sacrificial ritual. This apparently 'profligate' use of costly material is testimony to the importance attached to such rituals. Nowadays these bronze depositions – which are found primarily in watery locations, beside rivers and streams, and in marshes – are explained in terms of the 'cultural biography' of the object.[43] It is argued that in the cycle of production, circulation and deposition, bronze objects accrued meanings akin to personification or 'humanisation', because during their own lifetimes they had been closely associated with the life of an individual.[44] When, after long use, such objects were eventually laid to rest in the ground, as if they were living beings, their life cycle was fulfilled and at the same time the landscape took on a new, sacred significance. Is it here that the myth of the living bronze began?

The myths of bronze still resonate in its use today. 'Elmo', the enormous bronze helmet covered with mysterious runic symbols that Mimmo Paladino made in 1998, contains many echoes of the myths of bronze (Fig. 7). In one way, this work presents itself as a huge archaeological find, as the remnants of the armour of a gigantic primal warrior from a prehistoric age; at the same time, its basic form and inscriptions evoke associations with a great church bell like the one cast by Boriska. The inscriptions seem to hold the key to the identity of 'Elmo', but we cannot read and interpret them clearly. Paladino presents us with undecipherable messages, but in its very elusiveness the 'Elmo' evokes something of the mysterious nature of bronze. It seems to suggest that, even if we are no longer capable of fully understanding the original meanings of bronze objects, we can still sense their mythical, apotropaic qualities. The foundry may no longer be shrouded in secrets, but the ancient language of bronze continues to resonate in the modern objects that are fashioned from it.

Translated from the Dutch by *Lynne Richards*

NOTES

1 Cellini himself referred to 'courage' as an essential element in the successful casting of a bronze. See Cellini, *Life of Benvenuto Cellini* (trans. Symonds), p. 358 ('But if your Excellency goes on disheartening me') and p. 359 ('I took new courage').

2 Cellini tells us that he started by making the bust of Cosimo I de'Medici in order to gain experience with clay for the model and with casting in bronze. He also says that some jealous sculptors mockingly called him a 'new' sculptor; the 'Perseus' was to prove that Cellini really was a capable sculptor and not just a successful goldsmith, see Cellini, *Life of Benvenuto Cellini*, pp. 341–3 and p. 347. See also Cole, *Cellini*, p. 49.

3 Cellini, *Life of Benvenuto Cellini*, p. 363.

4 Cole, *Cellini*, p. 50 and p. 51.

5 Cellini, *Life of Benvenuto Cellini*, p. 364.

6 Kenneth Gross, *The dream of the moving statue*, Ithaca and London, 1992.

7 Eliade, *The forge*, pp. 34–42.

8 Eliade, *The forge*, p. 41 and p. 52.

9 Biringuccio, *Pirotechnia*, especially p. 13; see also Newman, *Promethean ambitions*, p. 51, p. 67 and pp. 127–32.

10 Kalbe, *Bergwerk und Probierbüchlein*.

11 Eliade, *The forge*, pp. 48–9.

12 Newman, *Promethean ambitions*, p. 105 (citing Raphael Aversa).

13 Newman, *Promethean ambitions*, pp. 78–82 and pp. 86–92.

14 In a woodcut by Dürer in Sebastian Brant's *Narrenschiff* (1494) the devil uses bellows to breathe evil deeds into mankind. Adriaen de Vries used bellows as an attribute in his 'Juggling Man', an allegory of hermetic wisdom, see *Adriaen de Vries* (1998), pp. 201–3 (no. 32).

15 Cole, *Cellini*, p. 51, citing the alchemist Antonio Allegretti, a friend of Cellini's; see also p. 58.

16 For the term 'lost lizard' process see Montagu, *Roman Baroque sculpture*, p. 54, note 22. See further Kris, 'Stil "Rustique"', pp. 136–208; Norberto Gramaccini, 'Das genaue Abbild der Natur, Riccios Tiere und die Theorie des Naturabgusses seit Cennino Cennini', in *Natur und Antike*, pp. 198–225.

17 Newman, *Promethean ambitions*, pp. 149–53 and pp. 164–237.

18 Exodus, books 8–10; Newman, *Promethean ambitions*, pp. 45–8 and p. 52.

19 Elizabeth Dalucas, 'Ars erit archetypus naturae, zur Ikonologie der Bronze in der Renaissance', in *Von allen Seiten schön*, pp. 70–81, especially p. 73.

20 *Adriaen de Vries* (1998), p. 189 (no. 27).

21 Eliade, *The forge*, pp. 25–9.

22 Newman, *Promethean ambitions*, p. 78; Biringuccio, *Pirotechnia*, p. 444.

23 Vulcan also contributed to the image of the sculptor as the artisan who did heavy, dirty work. That negative image was seized upon later by painters to give their profession greater eminence and lend it an aura of erudition at the expense of the status of sculptors. See James Hall, *The world as sculpture*, London, 1999, pp. 20–1.

24 Cole, *Cellini*, p. 49.

25 Hall (op. cit.), p. 22.

26 See Dalucas (op. cit.) in *Von allen Seiten schön*, p. 74 and Gramaccini, 'Zur Ikonologie der Bronze', pp. 147–70, especially p. 147.

27 Rosemarie Mulcahy in *Adriaen de Vries* (1998), p. 49 and p. 294.

28 Cellini, *Life of Benvenuto Cellini*, p. 342.

29 *Adriaen de Vries* (1998), p. 40.

30 *Von allen Seiten schön*, no. 45. Ostensibly or actually leaving a bronze unfinished may also be related to the growing interest in *bozzetti*, which were prized for their unpolished spontaneity and freshness. This trend is also indicative of the fascination with the process of creating a work of art that existed among collectors and patrons.

31 Butters, *Triumph of Vulcan*, vol. 1, pp. 242–5, and vol. 2, p. 460; Cellini, *Life of Benvenuto Cellini*, p. 344 and p. 358.

32 Lichtenberg, *Johan Gregor van der Schardt*, pp. 17–20.

33 *Adriaen de Vries* (1998), pp. 22–3. Almost a century before, Emperor Maximilian I also had tried to breathe new life into the art of bronze casting at his court by employing the ill-fated Gilg Sesselschreiber and his successor Stephan Godl. They were charged with making a magnificent tomb in the Hofkirche in Innsbruck.

34 *Adriaen de Vries* (1998), p. 23.

35 Rome had already been the example for Charlemagne, who saw himself as the heir to the old empire. His commissions for works in bronze derived from this political motivation and were intended to transform his seat of Aix-la-Chapelle into a new Rome. His lead was followed by Henry the Lion, Duke of Saxony and Bavaria, who had a monumental bronze lion erected in Brunswick in 1166. See Gramaccini, 'Zur Ikonologie der Bronze', p. 153, p. 157 and p. 161.

36 Raff, *Die Sprache der Materialien*, p. 97.

37 Gramaccini, 'Zur Ikonologie der Bronze', pp. 158–60.

38 See for example *Ruhm und Sinnlichkeit*, nos 9, 10, 12. The names given to cannon are often mildly facetious: 'Die schöne Katharina' (the beautiful Catherine) or 'Die Königin' (the Queen).

39 E. van Loon-Van de Moosdijk, '*Goet ende wael gheraect*', *versieringsmotieven op luid- and speelklokken uit Middeleeuwen en Renaissance in het hertogdom Brabant* (1300–1559), Nijmegen, 2004, pp. 159–60.

40 Moosdijk (op. cit.), p. 305 (no. 2).

41 Pliny, *Natural History*, Book XXXIV, iii, 5.

42 Fontijn, *Sacrificial landscapes*.

43 This term was introduced by Igor Kopytoff, 'The cultural biography of things: commoditization as process', in Arjun Appadurai, *The social life of things*, Cambridge 1986, pp. 64–91.

44 Fontijn, *Sacrificial landscapes*, pp. 25–36.

UNDER THE SIGN OF VULCAN

Michael W. Cole

WE ARE NOT ALWAYS accustomed to thinking about bronze sculpture in association with the cannon and armour this exhibition brings together. At least in the early modern period, however, objects such as these were bound by much more than their common material. The production of bronze 'artworks' was continuous with other industries, including the war industry, and this continuity manifested itself in various arenas. The present essay will highlight a number of these: patronage patterns, classification systems, models on which artists thought about themselves, professional paths that individuals who worked with bronze followed. A good place to begin, however, is with a figure that emblematised the links at issue: that of Vulcan, god of the forge.

Consider the 'Vulcan' Vincenzo de'Rossi made in the early 1570s for the *studiolo* of Duke Francesco I de'Medici in Florence (Figs 1 and 2). A bronze statuette, de'Rossi's piece would have advertised both the access Francesco had to a rare and valuable material, and the skills he had in his service. These two aspects of the piece, moreover, would have been amplified by the overall context of the room. In addition to its painted and sculpted decorations, the *studiolo* housed a

collection of natural 'treasures' or curiosities, organised thematically in cabinets within the walls, keyed to the four elements. The bronze statues, placed in niches at the tops of these walls, represented elemental deities, Vulcan himself serving as an 'inventor' and 'protector' of the treasures related to fire.[1] In situ, then, de'Rossi's 'Vulcan' would have represented all fiery things, materials such as gunpowder and glass, but also the bronze from which the statue itself was made.

Near the statue, and covering the cabinets holding the treasures, were to be paintings showing a bronze foundry, an alchemist's laboratory, a cannon factory, a goldsmith's shop and other workplaces that, taken together, further promoted Vulcan as the patron of a broad yet specific range of crafts – 'varieties of artifice', to use the phrase of Vincenzo Borghini, the *studiolo's* planner.[2] To the extent that the imagery of the *studiolo* can be said to be about works like de'Rossi's, that is, this was true in relation not only to the substance from which it was made, but also to the techniques used to shape it. That Vulcan himself, finally, was to be understood not only as a protector, but also as a kind of embodiment of such activities, was indicated by the god's *re*appearance in a painting meant to hang directly below de'Rossi's statue, probably covering the cabinet that contained small bronze objects (including bronze statuettes), Vittore Casini's 'Forge of Vulcan'. In the *studiolo*, in other words, Vulcan represented not only the element of fire per se – the origin of all bronze things – but also, and more specifically, the work that is done with heat.[3] Vulcan was associated with particular materials, bronze among them, but he also stood for what in the sixteenth century would have been called *pirotechnia*, the *art* of fire in all of its forms.

Such a conception of Vulcan helps explain why, just a few years before de'Rossi commenced his figure, his Florentine colleague Vincenzo Danti took up a related theme in a poem, his 'Capitolo against Alchemy': 'more wood and more coals did I burn in vain', Danti wrote, 'than that most ancient Sicilian smith fired in Etna'.[4] The 'Sicilian smith' Vulcan could figure in a poem on alchemy for the same reason that a goldsmith like Danti could write one: alchemists and smiths both practised pyrotechnics. The artist's basis for comparing himself to Vulcan, and for satirising what he calls 'alchemy', was no doubt his own experience as a bronze caster.[5] Danti wrote the capitolo after a series of failed attempts to establish his own metallurgic expertise in Florence: three tries at casting a colossal statue of Hercules and Antaeus for the Medici villa at Castello ended in disaster, his attempt at founding a bronze safe door for Cosimo's study came out badly, and even his nominally successful 'Moses' relief is riddled with flaws.[6] What is significant in the present context, however, is not Danti's success or failure, but rather that he could imagine the art he carried out at the forge in relation to what he called 'alchemy', and that in seeking poetic expression for this aspect of his own sculptural practice, it was to Vulcan that he turned.

The traditional mythological literature presented Vulcan primarily as a maker of famously artful weapons and armour – what, in early modern Italian and English, would have fallen into the broad category of 'arms' (*arme* or *armi*). The link that Danti's and de'Rossi's Vulcans suggested between art and arms would have struck contemporaries as specifically modern, but the associ-

Fig. 1 Vincenzo de'Rossi (1525–87),
'Vulcan', Palazzo Vecchio, Florence

Fig. 2 Studiolo of Francesco I de'Medici,
Palazzo Vecchio, Florence

ation was itself hardly novel. In Vanoccio Biringuccio's 1540 *De la Pirotechnia*, the most important sixteenth-century Italian treatise on the subject, the chapter entitled 'On the techniques and methods used to form figures, especially in bronze' follows directly after the chapter 'On the differences between cannon, and on their measurements' and directly before the chapter 'On the techniques and methods used to form cannon'.[7] The arrangement gives the impression that a discussion of metal artworks could arise naturally as an excursus in a discussion of guns. This would, in de'Rossi's day, have surprised no one – Cellini, a contemporary whose various writings count among our best Renaissance sources on the art of bronze casting, also claimed to be an expert in firearms, and much earlier, Leonardo's interests had already moved between the dynamics of a monumental cast (Fig. 3) and the dynamics of cannon.[8] Bronze sculpture, as a subfield of pyrotechnics, was closely bound up with the science of guns. What the figure of Vulcan added to this sense of 'field' was above all an attractive mythological image through which artists could imagine their work.

The appeal of such a figure was not limited to Italy. In fact, some of the finest independent bronze representations of the Roman fire god appeared in the North. The goldsmith Hans Jamnitzer, for example, placed Vulcan on a 1580 bronze plaquette (Fig. 4). Though his own image is based on a Romanising precedent, Cornelis Bos' print after Maerten van Heemskerck's 'Vulcan' of 1540, it is likely that the plaquette was made for Nuremberg buyers, for the most significant change Jamnitzer introduced into Bos' design was to remove Vulcan from his interior setting and to place him into a Düreresque northern woodland.[9] Comparably, Adriaen de Vries made a relief of 'Vulcan's Forge' (Fig. 5) in 1611, while he was working for the Holy Roman Emperor Rudolf II in Prague.[10] Like Jamnitzer's plaquette, it was an object that could indulge civic, regional, or even national pride, simultaneously depicting and embodying the wealth of the lands and the sophistication of the technologies at hand.[11] Nuremberg had long stood as one of the most important centres of the European copper industry and trade, famed well beyond its walls both for its bronze workshops and for its arsenals.[12] From Prague, similarly, Rudolf presided not only over his own local arsenal and, with de Vries, over one of Europe's most impressive statue-casting facilities, but also over some of the continent's major mining regions.[13]

The economic and geographic associations of Vulcan imagery must have lent particular meaning to metal artisanry. For if local interests could encourage the mythologisation of the copper and bronze crafts, implicitly comparing an artist's or patron's base of operation with the lands of the gods, such thinking carried craftsmen along with it, giving them a model in the figure who stood at the centre of these stories. As the conception of the *studiolo* suggests, and as the literature and imagery at which we have been looking further implies, the field of pyrotechnics already established goldsmithing as a sibling to artillery-production. And as goldsmiths were tempted to consider their professions in relation to Vulcan, or to conceive of their work as something carried out under his sign, it is worth asking whether Vulcan's mythical products did

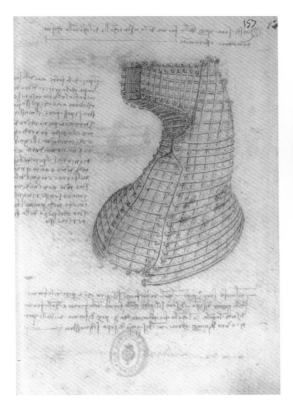

Fig. 4 Hans Jamnitzer (1539–1603),
'Vulcan', 1580, Germanisches
Nationalmuseum, Nuremberg

Fig. 3 Leonardo da Vinci (1452–1519),
Design for casting of the Sforza Horse,
1491, Biblioteca Nacional, Madrid

Fig. 5 Adriaen de Vries (1545–1626),
'Vulcan's Forge', 1611, Bayerisches
Nationalmuseum, Munich (detail)

not also become archetypes for the smith's. De'Rossi's 'Vulcan', like the Vulcans in Jamnitzer's plaquette and Heemskerck's painting, appears to be forging a lightning bolt.[14] This is certainly a glyph for the arts of fire, but it is also Jupiter's weapon. Similarly, the presence of Venus in both Jamnitzer's and de Vries' reliefs reminds us of Vulcan's other familiar products, the equipment he made, at Venus' bidding, for Mars and Aeneas.[15] In de Vries' panel, a helmet, cuirass and other arms lie about on the ground of the forge, but significantly the object of Vulcan's labours is left open-ended: are we to imagine that the plate he is hammering will become another piece of protective costume, or should we rather be reminded of relief sculptures like the very one in which this Vulcan finds himself?

The fact was that, even beyond the analogies that pyrotechnics supported, many of the products of goldsmiths like de Vries fell into the broad category covered by the early modern term 'arms'. We might think, for example, of another work de Vries made for Rudolf II, a 1603 portrait bust that set the emperor's head atop a cuirass (Fig. 6). The work gives the cuirass that appears in de Vries' Vulcan relief its own emblematic status, establishing a specific link between the work of the divine smith and de Vries himself. Thinking about the cuirass in the relief in this way, furthermore, does not just shed light on de Vries, for his portrait of Rudolf, as is well known, was commissioned to emulate the earlier busts Leone Leoni made depicting Emperor Charles V (Fig. 7).[16] De Vries' bust, that is, exemplifies a contemporary portrait *type*, one in which the artist made a number of essays and one in which, as he would have known, Leoni, too, specialised.

The professional model Leoni offered must have been important for de Vries. A goldsmith by training, the Italian artist had initially come into the service of Charles V in 1542 as a member of the imperial mint. After spending several years in Milan, however, Leoni began to pursue other types of commissions, above all large-scale portraits. Just what prompted Leoni, a die-maker then almost forty years old, to change his field of specialisation?[17] Leoni shared the period's passion for the colossal, as his collection of plaster casts after Michelangelo and the antique indicates, but professionally he may have been spurred by Cellini, his great rival, whose career had followed a similar trajectory. Likewise known in Italy primarily for his coins, Cellini undertook his first free-standing bronze cast in the form of a portrait (Fig. 8), one that showed its sitter, as the artist himself put it, '*armed* with al'antica spoils'.[18] That Leoni's own change of direction happened in Milan, moreover, is itself significant, for this city was one of the Italian peninsula's major centres for monumental casting. Milan hosted a famous armoury, and it was the only Italian city singled out by Biringuccio for its production of brass.[19] It was a city shadowed by the legend of Leonardo's attempt at making colossal bronzes, a place where Leoni could study the technology behind the large-scale pour and, more importantly, hire experts to assist him.

The works by Leoni we might classify as his 'armed portraits' – in addition to the Charles V bust, we might think here of his 1564 Gian Giacomo de'Medici tomb, or his 1588 portrait of Ferrante Gonzaga – fit into a longer-standing tradition, both north and south of the Alps, of

Fig. 6 Adriaen de Vries, Bust of
Rudolf II, 1603, Kunsthistorisches
Museum, Vienna

Fig. 7 Leone Leoni (c.1509–90),
Bust of Charles V, 1555,
Kunsthistorisches Museum, Vienna

Fig. 8 Benvenuto Cellini (1500–71),
Bust of Cosimo I, c.1545–48, Bargello,
Florence

sculpted figures in armour. Contemporaries must have realised, however, that something different happened when the increasing availability of metals began to allow sculptors to test the boundaries between actual protective costumes (whether in bronze or steel, for parade or for war), and metal representations of the same. Works like those just mentioned can be compared to sixteenth-century assemblages (Fig. 9) in which a head would be added to a suit of armour to generate the impression of a free-standing figure – or the impression of a *sculpture*. A polychromed silver head of Philip II (Fig. 10), modelled by Leoni's son and collaborator Pompeo, and preserved today in the Kunsthistorisches Museum in Vienna, was most likely made for insertion into a suit of armour, which was melted down in the late seventeenth century.[20] The conjunction can be seen from two points of view: the head of Philip may be a way of bringing the armour itself to life, but the format also allows the portrait to be reduced to its armour. If expediency demanded, heads could be exchanged or the armour left to stand on its own. When called upon to make an 'armed portrait', in turn, goldsmiths must have been faced with two tasks: to make a likeness of a person and a suggestive double of that person's 'arms'.

The Leoni family's most tantalising creation in the light of these themes is no doubt the 1555 bronze 'Charles V Restraining Fury' (Fig. 11). The textual source for the statue is a passage from Virgil's *Aeneid*, famous in the artist's day, that allegorised the end of war and the return of peace with the image of 'impious Furor, sitting on savage arms, his hands bound fast behind with a hundred bronze knots'.[21] The scene would have been familiar to the Leoni family, for Cellini had made a medal of the subject while he and Leone were competing for positions at the mint in Clement VII's Rome.[22] It is significant, moreover, that the Leoni statue, like Cellini's medal and the numerous subsequent medals based on it, includes a detail not present in Virgil, the *burning* of the weapons on which Furor sits.[23] The heaped weapons, on the verge of being melted, suggest that both artists were additionally thinking of the no less famous lines from Isaiah 2:4: 'and they shall turn their swords into ploughshares, and their spears into sickles'. As the *c.*1609 painting by Jan Brueghel and Hendrik van Balen (Fig. 12) reminds us, the agent who destroys the weapons could be the very one that Cellini shows: Peace itself. The operation the painting illustrates, of weapons feeding the forge, was one that both patrons and sculptors might reflect on.[24]

As far as patrons were concerned, such images might serve as reminders that bronze could as easily become weapons as statuary. The metal originally earmarked for Leonardo's Sforza monument was eventually turned into artillery, and the metal in Michelangelo's only bronze portrait met the same fate.[25] The Holy Roman emperors had to issue mandates banning the sale of copper objects to the Turks, knowing that they could be transformed into arms; the Turks, for their part, did the same.[26] The patrons of Augsburg's armoury, the one building in the city to bear enormous bronzes on its façade, made a point of this: Hans Reichle's monumental 1607 decorations (Fig. 13), no less than the inscription they accompany – '*belli instrumento pacis firmamento*' (to the instruments of war and the strengthening of peace) – indicate what goes on

Fig. 10 Pompeo Leoni (c.1533–1608),
Head of King Philip II of Spain, c.1556,
Kunsthistorisches Museum, Vienna

Fig. 9 Desiderius Helmschmid
(1513–c.1578), Coat of Armour
for Philip II of Spain, 1546,
Kunsthistorisches Museum, Vienna

Fig. 11 Leone Leoni, 'Charles V
Restraining Fury', 1555, Museo
Nacional del Prado, Madrid

Fig. 12 Jan Brueghel the Elder (1568–1625)
and Hendrik van Balen (c.1574/5–1632),
'Prophecy of The Prophet Isaiah',
c.1609, Alte Pinakothek, Munich

Fig. 13 Hans Reichle (c.1565/70–1642),
Bronze decorations, 1607, Zeughaus,
Augsburg

Fig. 14 Mattäus Gundelach
(c.1566–1654), 'Venus in Pygmalion's
Workshop', 1639, Gemäldegalerie Alte
Meister, Kassel

Fig. 15 Pietro Tacca (bapt. 1577–1640),
Equestrian monument to Ferdinand I,
1608, Florence

Fig. 16 Guglielmo della Porta (d. 1577),
Tomb of Paul III, 1575, St. Peter's Basilica,
Vatican State

inside the building. Brueghel's own painting is importantly ambiguous here: Peace torches the weapons, and the smiths make the ploughshares, but the pile of metalworks that bespeaks the abundance of the forge includes arms. The picture might remind us that any substantial use of bronze in statuary – and here it is the size as much as the subject of the bronzes that matters – was conspicuous both as metal and as talent that could have been (and could still be) put to other purposes.

Mattäus Gundelach's 1639 version of the Pygmalion theme (Fig. 14), also made in Augsburg, probably at the end of the Thirty Years War, pictures this point, showing Galatea as a statue of bronze rather than ivory, and surrounding the artist with, among other things, a bronze cannon and a copper bowl.[27] Sculptures themselves, however, could also announce this: on Pietro Tacca's 1608 equestrian monument of Francesco I (Fig. 15), in the piazza in front of the SS. Annunziata in Florence, the giant horse wears an inscription across its broad belly: *'Dei metalli rapiti al fero Trace'* (made of metals taken from the fierce Thracians).[28] The art is a testament not only to the defeat of Turkish armies, but also to the destruction of enemy arms, and thus to the peace the ruler represented. In Rome, the 1614 bronze Virgin on the column in front of the church of Sta Maria Maggiore, holding the Prince of Peace, was cast from weapons.[29] It is possible that Paul V, the reigning Pope at the time, was thinking here of his namesake Paul III (Fig. 16), who elected to have his 1575 tomb-portrait, which shows him in the pose of a 'peacemaker', made in bronze.[30] Similar conceits can be found right into modern times: the reliefs around the Vendôme column in Paris, for example, commissioned by Napoleon I, were cast from cannon captured at the battle of Austerlitz in 1805; and in 1833, Leo von Klenze's obelisk in Karolinenplatz, Munich, commemorating soldiers killed in Napoleon's Russian campaign of 1812, was cast from captured Russian, Austrian and French weapons, as well as discarded Bavarian bronze cannon.[31]

For makers of statues, of course, both the alternative uses to which metals could be put and the similar operations that underlay them mattered as well. Leonardo had studied cannon manufacture in preparation for casting the Sforza monument; Leoni, to cast his statues, needed not only bronze in quantity, but also the advice and probably the assistance of the cannon-makers themselves; Cellini, de Vries and others all either brought such professionals into their workshops or entered the workshops of the cannon-makers once they began to take on more monumental commissions.[32] Goldsmiths represented a special case. As experts in metals, many eventually found it possible to carry out their own bronze casts, and even to pursue work as cannon makers, as Danti, for example, was doing by 1571.[33] More generally, the confluence of professional paths enriched the connotations of the crafts that any goldsmith might employ. The juxtaposition of bronze figures and bronze weapons in the Leoni 'Charles V Restraining Fury' or Reichle's armoury group underscores the continuity between the production of arms and statues. Here we might think about what the Leoni have actually made – not the weapons that were sometimes destroyed to make sculptures, but new, if fictional, arms: in composing the bases for their figures, the Leoni forged swords, tridents, and battle horns.[34] And in what has, from Vasari's day to ours, been considered the most virtuoso aspect of the portrait, the Leoni provided the emperor with a *removable* suit of mail.[35] The inevitable question here is whether the real interest of the work is its ostensible theme – the destruction of weapons in celebration of Peace (whose role the emperor ostensibly plays) – or its unmistakable demonstration, that the coin- and statue-maker could actually produce arms.[36]

As John Hayward and others have amply documented, goldsmiths were, in their way, arms-makers: their products could include complete suits of armour (Leoni, for one, made not only the apparently artful mail for his Charles V, but also a real suit of armour for Ferrante Gonzaga, the governor of Milan), as well as weapons.[37] Andrea Riccio, Wenzel Jamnitzer, Erasmus Mornick and Daniel Hopfer all made or worked on swords, and Cellini tells us that his skills as a goldsmith allowed him not only to decorate hilts, but to manufacture real blades, sharp enough for a surgeon to use.[38] When the time came to equip his own 'Perseus', Cellini did not use bronze, but worked a separate piece in iron, making the sword as a real weapon.[39] The armaments Cellini made for his figures might be compared to those that Leoni, Reichle and others forged, some but not all of them props.

The specific skills inculcated by a goldsmith's training allowed him to insinuate himself into the war industry. John Hayward, for example, draws attention to the requirements of coin-making; the knowledge of cutting hard steel dies could be used to work on the base metals of armour.[40] In some cases, the skills employed for sculptures in bronze could lead artists into more dangerous pursuits. A dramatic illustration of this possibility is provided by the life of Bartolomeo Campi. The son of a goldsmith, Campi began his career in the same profession, making medals through the 1540s.[41] What really established his fame, however, was not a coin but a suit of armour (Fig. 17), which he made in 1546 (the same year that Leoni and Cellini began making their armed portraits), and which the Duke of Urbino subsequently gave to Charles V. Although the signature on the armour indicates that Campi understood even this as a product of goldsmithery, the work launched him on an adventurous itinerary. By the 1550s Campi had left his native Pesaro to work as a military engineer in Venice and Siena; by the 1560s he was working for King Henry II, designing new weapons, presumably cannon (his brother Giacomo had been casting cannon in Florence since at least 1555). Eventually, Emperor Philip II sent him north as a military advisor. Beginning in 1568 he was involved in designing fortifications; he died at the siege of Haarlem in 1573.[42]

Campi, to be sure, represents an extreme case: seldom did it happen that the goldsmith's trade actually led him into battle. Sculptors did their best business in peacetime, in no small part because that was when materials were available to them. They can only have been aware, moreover, that the material and even the very production of bronze figures enabled works as diverse in form and genre as della Porta's 'Paul III' (Fig. 16), Tacca's equestrian portrait, and

Reichle's 'St. Michael' to make peace part of their message. At the same time, a clientele of warriors and a studio stocked with arms must have seemed to promise an expansion of the goldsmith's craft to the level of myth. Working under the sign of Vulcan, the goldsmith came to the edge of the fierce world that the demigod himself occupied.

Fig. 17 Bartolomeo Campi (c.1500–73), Armour, 1546, Armeria Real, Madrid

NOTES

1 See Borghini, reprinted in Ettore Allegri and Alessandro Cecchi, *Palazzo Vecchio e i Medici: Guida Storico*, Florence, 1980, p. 342: 'però havea pensato che tutte questa inventione fusse dedicata alla natura et all'arte, mettendoci statue che rappresentino quelli che furno o inventori o cagione, o (come credette l'antica poesia) tutori et preposti a' tesori della natura, et historie di pittura che mostrino anche loro la varietà et l'artificio di quelle'.

2 For the most recent bibliography on the various reconstructions of the room, see Larry Feinberg, 'The studiolo of Francesco I reconsidered', in Christina Acidini Lichinat et al., *The Medici, Michelangelo, & the art of late Renaissance Florence*, New Haven and London, 2002, pp. 47–65.

3 Compare also Borghini in Allegri and Cecchi (op. cit.), p. 342, who treats fire as an 'operator', as opposed to air and water, which are more 'material'.

4 See Danti's 'Capitolo contro l'Alchimia del q[ua]le ogni terzo verso è del Petrarca', in Summers, *Vincenzo Danti*, pp. 505–12.

5 In Danti's day, the term *alchimia* could denote much the same range of arts as *pirotechnia*. See Varchi, *Questione*.

6 See Summers, *Vincenzo Danti*, as well as Charles Davis, 'Working for Vasari: Vincenzo Danti in Palazzo Vecchio', in Gian Carlo Gafagnini, ed., *Giorgio Vasari tra decorazione ambientale e storiografia artistica*, Florence, 1985, pp. 205–71.

7 See Vannoccio Biringuccio, *De la pirotechnia* (1540), ed. Adriano Carugo, Milan (facs. ed.), 1977 (see bibliography for English translation).

8 For Leonardo's pyrotechnics see W. Chandler Kirwin, 'The bubble reputation: in the cannon's and the horse's mouth (or, the tale of three horses)', in Ahl, *Leonardo*, pp. 87–110. For Cellini's skill with guns, see *The life of Benvenuto Cellini*, trans. Robert H. Hobart Cust, 2 vols, London, 1910, vol. 1, pp. 94–5 and pp. 133–6.

9 For Jamnitzer see *Wenzel Jamnitzer* (1985), p. 433 (nos 566–7). Another example of the plaquette can be found in the National Gallery of Art in Washington. Two earlier Vulcan plaquettes, both ascribed to Andrea Riccio, are in the National Gallery in Washington, and an early sixteenth-century freestanding statuette of Vulcan, which Planiscig ascribed to Riccio, is in the Martin Le Roy collection in Paris. See Leo Planiscig, *Venezianische Bildhauer der Renaissance*, Vienna, 1921, p. 138 (fig. 148). For the Heemskerk painting and the Bos print based on it, see especially Ilja M. Veldman, *Maarten van Heemskerck and Dutch humanism in the sixteenth century*, trans. Michael Hoyle, Amsterdam, 1977, pp. 21–42 (illustrated p. 23, fig. 5); I owe thanks to Larry Silver for this reference.

10 For de Vries' panel see the entry in *Adriaen de Vries* (1998), pp. 187–9.

11 The typical presence of Venus in these reliefs is licensed by her prominent role in the Vulcan myth. Since the mining literature traditionally associated copper with Venus, however, it is also possible that her presence indicates something further, namely, the generative source of the material Vulcan works. Compare, for example, the role given to Venus in the *Nützlich Bergbüchlein*, Erfurt, 1527, chapter 1 (attributed to Ulrich Rülein von Kalbe; see bibliography for English translation).

12 Hermann Kellenbenz, 'Europäisches Kupfer, Ende 15. bis Mitte 17. Jahrhundert: Ergebnisse eines Kolloquiums', and Othmar Pickl, 'Kupfererzeugung und Kupferhandel in den Ostalpen', both in Kellenbenz, *Schwerpunkte*, pp. 290–351 and pp. 117–47; see also Hermann Kellenbenz, *The rise of the European economy: an economic history of Continental Europe from the fifteenth to the eighteenth century*, London, 1976, p. 109.

13 On the copper mines of Bohemia see Ferber, *Beyträge*.

14 Other comparable examples might be cited here, including the monumental Vulcan on Hubert Gerhard's early seventeenth-century Wittelsbacher Fountain.

15 Aeneas is in Virgil, *Aeneid*, 8.423–53.

16 The basic discussion is Larsson, *Adrian de Vries*, pp. 36–8.

17 Even after Leoni's death, writers described him professionally as 'il coniatore' (the die-maker). See for example Paolo Morigi, *La Nobiltà di Milano*, Milan, 1619, p. 67, cited in Michael Mezzatesta, 'Imperial themes in the sculpture of Leone Leoni', unpublished doctoral dissertation, New York University, 1980, p. 240.

18 Emphasis mine. See Cole, *Cellini*, p. 184, n. 24. Leoni uses similar language in a letter to Ferrante Gonzaga: see Giuseppe Campori, *Gli Artisti italiani e stranieri negli stati estensi*, Bologna (fasc. ed.), 1969, p. 290; also cited in Mezzatesta (op. cit.), p. 451.

19 Biringuccio (op. cit.). See also Hermann Kellenbenz, 'Production and trade of gold, silver, copper, and lead from 1450 to 1750', in Kellenbenz and Schneider, *Precious metals*, pp. 307–61.

20 See the entry by M.a Luisa Tárraga in *Los Leoni (1509–1608): escultores del Renacimiento italiano al servicio de la corte de España* (exhibition catalogue), Prado, Madrid, 1994, p. 138.

21 Virgil, 1.294–6.

22 For Cellini's medal, see most recently Beth Holman, 'For "Honor and Profit": Benvenuto Cellini's "Medal of Clement VII" and His Competition with Giovanni Bernardi', *Renaissance Quarterly* 68 (2005): 512–75, with further references.

23 Similar details are included in the 'Peace' Leone Leoni made for the tomb of Gian Giacomo dei Medici (Milan, Cathedral), in the *sportello* Vincenzo Danti made for Duke Cosimo I de'Medici (Florence, Bargello), in the 'Peace' Jacopo Sansovino made for the Campanile in Piazza San Marco in Venice, and on the versos of numerous contemporary medals.

24 On the image, see Ingrid Jost, 'Hendrick van Balen der Älter: Versuch einer Chronologie der Werke aus den ersten zwei Jahrzehnten des siebzehnten Jahrhunderts unter besonderer Berücksichtigung der Kabinettsbilder', *Nederlands Kunsthistorisch Jaarboek*, 14, 1963, pp. 83–128 (especially pp. 119–20).

25 For the fate of Leonardo's metal see Carlo Pedretti, 'The Sforza horse in context', in Ahl, *Leonardo*, pp. 27–39 (especially p. 32).

26 See the excellent discussion in Josef Vlachović, 'Die Kupfererzeugung und der Kupferhandel in der Slowakei vom Ende des 15. bis zur Mitte des 17. Jahrhunderts', Kellenbenz, *Schwerpunkte*, pp. 148–71.

27 For the Gundelach painting, see *Pygmalions Werkstatt: die Erschaffung des Menschen im Atelier von der Renaissance bis zum Surrealismus* (exhibition catalogue), ed. Helmut Friedel, Cologne, 2001, pp. 194–5 (no. 70).

28 The inscription is still easily legible on the underside of the horse. See also Baldinucci's comments on the episode, *Notizie dei professori del disegno da cimabue in qua*, ed. F. Ranalli, Florence, 1846, vol. 2, p. 577.

29 Steven Ostrow, 'Paul V, the Column of the Virgin and the new *Pax Romana*', article in progress.

30 For the significance of the gesture Guglielmo della Porta's 'Paul' makes, see Julian Kliemann, 'L'immagine di Paolo III come pacificatore: osservazioni sul "salotto dipinto"', in Catherine Monbeig Goguel, ed., *Francesco Salviati et la Bella Maniera*, Rome, 2001, pp. 287–310.

31 Gamboni, *The destruction of art*; *Leo von Klenze: Architekt zwischen Kunst und Hof 1784–1864* (exhibition catalogue), Münchner Stadtmuseum, Munich, 2000.

32 On the Cellini see, most recently, Cole, *Cellini*, p. 48; for the situation in Munich, see Dorothea Diemer, 'Bronzeplastik um 1600 in München: neue Quellen und Forschungen', *Jahrbuch des Zentralinstituts für Kunstgeschichte*, 2, 1986, pp. 107–77; for Giambologna see Sabine Eiche, 'Giambologna's Neptune Fountain in Bologna: newly-discovered letters from 1565', *Mitteilungen des Kunsthistorischen Instituts in Florenz*, 1994, pp. 428–9; and Mary Weitzel Gibbons, 'Documents concerning Giambologna's equestrian monument of Cosimo I, a bronze crucifix and the marble centaur', *Burlington Magazine*, 1978, pp. 508–10; for de Vries see Francesca Bewer, 'The sculpture of Adriaen de Vries: a technical study', in Pincus, *Small bronzes*, pp. 158–93; for Bernini see W. Chandler Kirwin, *Powers matchless: the Pontificate of Urban VIII, the Baldachin, and Gian Lorenzo Bernini*, New York, 1997. Leoni writes that, when he cast the 'Charles V', that the *capitano di giustizia* came to watch the event. It is tempting to ask whether this indicates the general appeal of such a spectacle to those with a professional interest in weapons; see Eugène Plon, *Les maîtres italiens au service de la maison d'Autriche. Leone Leoni, sculpteur de Charles-Quint, et Pompeo Leoni, sculpteur de Philippe II*, Paris, 1887, p. 95.

33 For Danti as a cannon founder, see Giovan Battista Fidanza's entry in Günther Meissner, ed., *Allgemeines Künstlerlexikon*, Munich, 1992-present, vol. 24, p. 213.

34 Leoni himself referred to the objects grouped at Charles' feet generically as 'arms' (*armi*); see Plon (op. cit.), p. 362.

35 See Gaetano Milanesi, ed., *Le vite de'piu eccellenti pittori, scultori ed architettori*, Florence, 1880, VII, p. 536. Leoni suggested that, with this device, it would be possible to 'arm and disarm' his statue; see Plon (op. cit.), p. 367.

36 Hayward, *Virtuoso goldsmiths*, pp. 313–30.

37 For goldsmiths as makers of armour, see Hayward, *Virtuoso goldsmiths*. For Leoni's armour, see the entry on Leoni in the *Dizionario biografico degli Italiani*, Roma, 1960–present, *ad vocem*.

38 For Hopfer see Anthony F. Radcliffe, 'Ricciana', *Burlington Magazine*, 1982, pp. 412–24, and Wolfgang Wegner, 'Ein Schwert von Daniel Hopfer im Germanischen Nationalmuseum in Nürnberg', *Münchner Jahrbuch der Bildenden Kunst*, 1954, pp. 124–30. For Cellini see Cust (op. cit.), pp. 185–6.

39 John Pope-Hennessy, *Cellini*, New York, 1985, p. 186.

40 Hayward, *Virtuoso goldsmiths*, pp. 324–5.

41 For Campi's career, see *Allgemeines Künstlerlexikon* (op. cit.) and the *Dizionario Biografico* (op. cit.).

42 For Campi's projects for defensive architecture see Charles van den Heuvel, 'Bartolomeo Campi successor to Francesco Paciotto in the Netherlands. A different method of designing citadels: Groningen and Flushing', in Marino Viganò, ed., *Architetti e ingegneri militari italiani*, Livorno, 1994, vol. 1, pp. 153–67.

ROOM ONE

ORIGINS AND PROPERTIES

INTRODUCTION

In an ink sketch of around 1510, Leonardo da Vinci depicts a downpour of household objects and the artisan's tools required to make them, falling like rain from the sky (Fig. 1). His image, on the one hand, portrays a deluge of material goods, but on the other, it connects man-made things to heaven and the elements, and reminds us that objects embody creative impulses which often remain invisible. Since earliest times, metals were closely identified with planets and gods; the copper and tin of bronze, for example, with Venus and Jupiter. Found in nature, metals manifested the spiritual on earth, lending a mystical dimension to metal-working. The fusion of metals to create alloys, which are not usually found in nature, suggests an alchemical transformation of matter. The work of the smith, the founder, and the alchemist thus represented not only technical skill, but esoteric knowledge and a profound understanding of the workings of nature.

The first room of the exhibition brings together a number of objects that communicated these beliefs through their function and use. Fulfilling a variety of roles within different interiors, bronze was experienced directly, through touch, in a more or less private capacity. Even a communal ritual – such as lighting an incense burner during mass – involved a personal connection with the material. Through their design and function, such objects acted as metaphorical devices for representing spiritual enlightenment. The oil contained in a lamp or the sound that resides in a bell was like an inner spirit that became animated when the object was used.

Fig. 1 Leonardo da Vinci (1452–1519), ink drawing showing a rain of material possessions, c.1510

Many of the functions and rituals of bronze are of a timeless nature, and we still recognise and identify with objects that are hundreds of years old. The simple design of an incense burner, for example, has remained largely unchanged from antiquity to the present day, as examples dating from the second, sixteenth and nineteenth centuries show (Cat. 19, 21 and 25). Certain types of objects immediately communicate an aspect of the physical character of bronze: aquamaniles and oil lamps indicate that bronze is impermeable and resistant to moderate heat, bells and door-knockers demonstrate its capacity for sound, mortars and cannon highlight its robustness and relative solidity. Although representing diverse functions, such objects are related by virtue of their material, a connection that is reflected in the methods of their production. Historically, mortars,

CHURCH BELLS AND HAND BELLS

bells and cannon were produced in the same foundries (Fig. 2) and bronze workers embodied a variety of roles; they could be bell founders and goldsmiths, as well as alchemists and weapons engineers. In their exacting knowledge of the material, the professions of bronze were as interchangeable as the objects produced, and their meanings were fluidly carried across from one to the other.

Fig. 2 A. Hotin, from Henry Havard, *Les Bronzes d'Art et d'Ameublement,* Librarie Charles Delagrave, Paris, no date, before 1900

In early modern communities, church bells formed an integral part of daily life, regulating the working day, announcing deaths and weddings, and calling worshippers to mass. The ring of the bell carried far and wide, not only symbolising but audibly enforcing the authority of the church: the command to worship was imposed on everyone, even those who would prefer not to. In Andrei Tarkovsky's film *Andrei Rublev* (1966), the deep symbolic value of the church bell is compellingly reflected in the immense resources and labour invested in its making (see Frits Scholten Fig. 1). Like a penance, every step of the process demanded physical exertion, from digging the casting pit, carting clay uphill to make the massive mould, building the great furnaces, and logging the wood that heats them. While the bell itself becomes a symbol of the conflict between power and religion, the film also suggests that bronze has a spiritual power of its own; dangerous, mysterious and utterly demanding, the material of the bell has an inner energy that lies beyond the grasp of any human authority. To make bronze sonorous was to awaken its soul, indicating not only the technical skill of the founder, but his profound understanding of the nature of metals. Tarkovsky's bell founder has learnt technical control over bronze, but the secret of how to make it ring died with his father. His bell turns out to be beautiful, but he knows it will not ring true; its inner spirit cannot be bought with silver.

The notion that the ring of the bell draws a line of communication between heaven and earth was not an invention of the modern church, but originates in much earlier ideas about the universal harmony of the heavenly spheres. Pythagoras is said to have discovered the principles of musical harmony when passing by a forge, and hearing the different sounds of hammers striking anvils. Franchino Gafori's image of Pythagoras' *Theorica Musice* (Fig. 3) likens the striking of anvils to the striking of bells, arranged on a musical scale, reminding us that it is the metallic composition of bells that determines their tone. Often the spiritual associations of bells are only implicit, but the hand bell of Emperor Rudolf II (Cat. 5), said to be composed of the seven metals of antiquity, overtly exhibits the astrological and heavenly associations of the metals in its decorative programme (Fig. 4). The metals – gold, which was linked to the sun, copper to Venus, quicksilver to Mercury, silver to the Moon, lead to Saturn, tin to Jupiter, and iron to Mars – are represented by their planetary symbols and the signs of the zodiacs they rule.

Fig. 3 Franchino Gafori, 'Pitagora' (Pythagoras) from *Theorica musice*, Mediolani, Milan 1492

Fig. 4 Cat. 5 (detail)

1

Gherijt Butendiic and Willem Sloterdiic
(active c.1450)
Bell
Netherlands; 1453
Bronze
Height: 70 cm, Diameter: 64 cm
Rijksmuseum, Amsterdam (BK-KOG-1956)

2

Probably Workshop of Gaspare di Girolamo Macri
(active c.1550)
Hand Bell showing an heraldic shield,
possibly the Arms of the Rossi family
Italy (Venice); early 16th century
Bronze with red silk tassel attached
Height: 10.3 cm, Diameter: 9.5 cm
Victoria and Albert Museum, London (M.28-1923)

3

Jan van der Eynde

(*fl.* second half 17th century)

Bell

With inscription:

ANTWERPIAE FECIT ME JOHANNES A FINE A 1550

(Johannes made me in Antwerp at the end of 1550)

Belgium (Antwerp); 1550

Bronze

Height: 16.4 cm, Diameter: 12.9 cm

Victoria and Albert Museum, London (M.99-1920)

4

Giuseppe de Levis (1552–1611/14)

Bell

Italy (Verona); 1583

Bronze

Height: 15.5 cm, Diameter: 10.4 cm

Victoria and Albert Museum, London (A.7-1987)

5

Hans Bulla

So-called 'Hand Bell of Emperor Rudolf II'

Bohemia (Prague); *c.*1600

Alloy of the classic seven metals (gold, copper, quicksilver, silver, lead, tin, iron); gold plated; iron clapper

Height: 7.8 cm, Diameter: 6.3 cm

Kunsthistorisches Museum, Vienna, Kunstkammer (KK 5969)

6
Samuel Smith
Bell
England (York); 1687
Bronze
Height: 63 cm, Diameter: 61 cm
Leeds Museums & Galleries,
Temple Newsam House

7
Jan Crans (1670–1739)
Bell
With inscription: IAN CRANS ME FECIT AO 1711
(Jan Crans made me in 1711)
Netherlands (Amsterdam); 1711
Bronze
Height: 17.5 cm, Diameter: 15 cm
Rijksmuseum, Amsterdam (BK-NM-10599)

MORTARS

The mortar not only demonstrates a range of different contexts in which bronze was used, it highlights the connections between them. In Stradanus' view into an alchemist's laboratory (Fig. 5) an apprentice is using a countersprung pestle to pound herbs in a large mortar, not unlike that in the V&A's collection (Cat. 10). Similar mortars were used in pharmacies, and smaller ones with hand-held pestles were found in kitchens, painters' studios, or anywhere where substances were ground and mixed together.[1] Although to different ends, mortars in all these contexts essentially served a kind of alchemy: changing and mixing substances to generate new ones. Indeed, Stradanus presents the mortar as the first stage of the alchemical work. Situated prominently in the foreground, the mortar initiates the cycle of transformation and exchange that unfolds around it in the laboratory. Bundles of firewood lie about, and an apprentice blows air into the fire with bellows; the heat generates condensation and clouds of vapour rise from the distilling apparatuses, a series of stages that represent the controlled interaction of the elements, as Stradanus reiterates: 'Distillation. In the fire, the juice of all bodies is turned by art into a mighty billow, clear and most potent'.[2]

The word mortar also refers to a type of short cannon, and both sorts of object were cast in the same foundry, along with bells, turning the mortar-shape upside down. In the image of 'gun powder' in the *Nova Reperta* (Fig. 6), Stradanus not only reminds us of the visual similarity of the two types of mortar, he makes an alchemical link in their function: the vignette above the furnace represents Berthold Schwartz, the legendary inventor of gun powder, at work in an alchemist's studio equipped with two mortars, while in the distance beyond, we see a city being destroyed by cannon-fire.[3]

Heraldic emblems and inscriptions sometimes indicated the name of the owner or pharmacy, but the ornamentation cannot always be interpreted with precision. The lizards decorating the V&A and Fitzwilliam mortars were cast from nature, and suggest a symbolic extension of the objects' alchemical associations (see also Cat. 11, 14 and 15).

OPPOSITE
Figs 5 and 6 Théodore Galle, after Jan van der Straet (Stradanus), 'Découvertes récentes. 07 La distillation' and '03 La poudre à canon', from *Nova Reperta*, Antwerp, *c.*1600

NOTES

1 See Motture, *Bells & mortars*; Matthew, *Antiques of the pharmacy*.
2 Translations cited here are from Bern Dibner's edition, in the Dibner Library, Smithsonian Institution, Washington DC; Straet (Stradanus), *Nova reperta*.
3 Ibid.

DISTILLATIO.
7. In igne ſuccus omnium, arte, corporum   Vigens fit vnda, limpida et potiſſima.

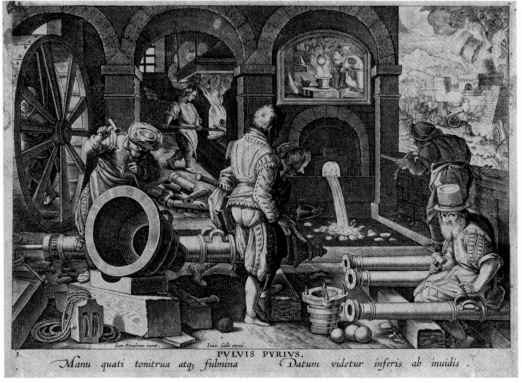

PVLVIS PYRIVS.
3. Manu quati tonitrua atq̃ fulmina   Datum videtur inferis ab inuidis.

8

Attributed to Alessandro Leopardi (*fl.*1482–1522)

Mortar with Lizard

Italy (Venice); *c*.1500

Bronze

Height: 14.5 cm, Diameter: 15.5 cm at lip,

10.4 cm at base

The Fitzwilliam Museum, Cambridge (M.18-1979)

9

Original plaquettes by Peter Flötner (*c*.1485–1546)

Mortar decorated with reliefs cast from plaquettes, with Pride, Hope and an allegory of a man and woman being led astray by Cupid

Southern Germany; *c*.1550

Bronze

Height: 12.3 cm, Diameter: 16.7 cm

Victoria and Albert Museum, London (M.16-1939)

9 (detail)

10 (detail)

10

Cast by Ambrogio Lucenti (d.1656)
Mortar with heraldic crest, lion rampant and bend,
with lizard and leaf decoration and inscription
around the rim in Latin:

SIMANDIVS DE TOTIS VRBEVETANVS CIVIS
ROMANVS ANNO D M D CXLII FECIT +

(Simandio de Toti (or Tozzi) of Orvieto,
citizen of Rome. Made 1642)
Italy (Rome); 1642
Bronze
Height: 33.4 cm,
Diameter: 43.43 cm at lip,
25.4 cm at base
Victoria and Albert Museum,
London (A.2-1974)

NATURE CASTING

The fascination with nature – the desire not only to study it but to imitate and even better it – is exemplified by the bronze life cast, which was known in antiquity but of which the most abundant examples passed down to us come from the fifteenth and sixteenth centuries. To make such casts, lizards, crabs and other creatures were killed in a way that minimised visible damage to their bodies (such as by drowning in an acidic solution); using string and other props, the creature was arranged in a pose, often artfully imitating their natural manner, and then covered in a plaster mix. For a direct cast, the body would be destroyed by the liquid metal, resulting in a unique solid cast; more commonly, the plaster would first be fired to burn out the body and create a mould, which could then be used for multiple hollow casts.[1]

As Frits Scholten also tells us (p. 26), some of these objects, in particular crabs and frogs, served as boxes and inkwells; others, such as lizards, were not obviously functional, although they may have been used as paperweights and also appear as decorations incorporated into other objects (see Cat. 8, 9 and 10). But their significance surely lay in the symbolic value of their naturalistic appearance. Reproducing the living creature in its most minute details and textures, such precise recordings of the natural world were perhaps only known elsewhere from fossilised remains. But unlike fossils, the creatures transferred into bronze were neither skeletal nor compressed, nor were they created naturally through the passing of time. They were the artificial products of manual art, and as such can be read as metaphors for the artist's relationship with nature.[2]

The process of casting from life suggests a sacrificial exchange between art and nature; the artist presides over a technical process that relies on nature's forms. But while his role might therefore be described more as an agent or facilitator than an inventor, the resulting object provides a visual manifestation of his reverence for the natural world. Transformed into bronze, the reptile or crab becomes a signifier of the mysteries of nature, a reminder that even the lowliest of creatures contain the force of life. Side by side, the two crabs reveal their individual character, demonstrating the uniqueness of each living creature. The insects and naturalia under the rim of a mortar (see Cat. 9) represent the minutiae that might live under stones or in debris; re-created in a precious metal, they reveal the exalted grace that resides in all living things.

In their exacting faithfulness to the living creature, these casts remind us of the most fundamental condition of bronze: that it is always essentially reproductive. Although it can take on almost any given shape, bronze is itself innately formless; it has no 'original' form, or even a raw state, and can be manipulated only indirectly, when poured into a mould as a liquid. Bronze, therefore, is always a copy of something else already in existence, such as a man-made model of clay or wax, or a living animal. But bronze is also generative, and we can think of the life cast as a kind of embodiment, or an alchemical metamorphosis, where one substance is transformed into another. The lizard, like its mythical cousin the salamander, was itself an alchemical symbol (Fig. 7).[3] Salamanders were thought to live and regenerate in fire, a notion literally embodied through the process of nature casting; as the body of the lizard is charred in fire, its image is reincarnated in bronze.

Fig. 7 'Purifying Gold presented by
the image of a salamander in the fire',
Emblem 10 from Adrian von
Mynsicht, *Dyas chymica tripartita*,
Frankfurt am Main, 1625

NOTES

1 For a brief description see *Die Beschwörung des Kosmos*.
2 See in particular Smith, *The body of the artisan*; also
Newman, *Promethean ambitions*.
3 Represented in Emblem 10 of *The Book of Lambspring*, the
accompanying poem states that 'the Salamander is born in

the fire', and even if it is killed, this 'happens for its good: /
For from its blood it wins immortal life / And then death
has no more power over it. / Its blood is the most precious
Medicine upon earth … / For this blood drives away all
disease / In the bodies of metals / Of men, and of beasts'.
Nicolas Barnaud, *The book of Lambspring*.

11
Gecko
Italy; *c.*15th–16th century
Bronze
Length: 9.3 cm
Staatliche Museen, Kassel (A.I. IX G 40)

12
Inkwell in the form of a Crab
Italy (Padua); beginning of the 16th century
Bronze
6 x 19 x 13 cm
Kunsthistorisches Museum, Vienna, Kunstkammer
(5927)

13
Small Crab
Italy (Padua); beginning of the 16th century
Bronze
7 x 13 x 9 cm
Kunsthistorisches Museum, Vienna, Kunstkammer
(5922)

14
Lizard
Italy (Padua?); 16th century
Bronze
4 x 7.5 x 26 cm
Staatliche Museen, Kassel (A.I. IX H 12)

15
Two Lizards
Italy; second half of the 16th century
Bronze
Length: 17.5 cm
Bayerisches Nationalmuseum, Munich (R 3572)

HAND OF SABAZIOS

Representing the right hand of a pair in the collection of the Louvre, this tiny but intricate object is bedecked with an array of figures and symbols identified with the cult of Sabazios (also known as Sabazius), god of the Phrygians, whose image is personified in the other hand (Fig. 8). The head of Mercury, a pine cone, a snake, lizard and other naturalia are grouped around the hand, its fingers arranged in a gesture of benediction. A plate from Bernard de Montfaucon's monumental catalogue of classical antiquities of 1722 (Fig. 9) shows that while several of these hands were known to exist, their iconography is individually specific. De Montfaucon depicts hands with symbols that overlap with, but do not exactly duplicate those of the two hands in the Louvre collection. The complexity of these objects re-flects the problems we encounter when we try to interpret mythological images. Their meanings are so diffuse and changeable, and their origins so obscure, that we can only guess at the precise significance they might have once had. But while we may lack the key to decipher their original meanings and connections, we can nonetheless sense the talismanic power with which they were invested. Echoing symbols presented in other contexts in this exhibition – Mercury, the serpent, the lizard – Sabazios' amulets seem to flow in and out of the hand spontaneously, as though liable to metamorphose into other forms, or to sink back and disappear into the bronze at any moment.

Fig. 8 'Sabazios wearing Phrygian cap', 3rd century BC, bronze, Musée du Louvre, Paris (Br 4310)

Fig. 9 From Bernard de Montfaucon, *L'Antiquité expliquée* (Paris, 10 vols, 1719 and 5 vols Supplement, 1724), vol. 2, part 2, plate 137, no. 4

16
Hand of Sabazios
Italy; 3rd century AD
Bronze
12.1 x 6.1 x 3.9 cm
Musée du Louvre, Paris, Durand Collection (Br 836)

DOORKNOCKER

Widely reproduced during the Renaissance with variant symbolic imagery, doorknockers such as this example, of Hercules with lions, seem to have been traditional in Venice, where they would have been found on the doors of palaces and monasteries. Here, the figure of Hercules, flanked by two lions, presents a recognisable symbol of strength and physical power, with the visual suggestion of the lion's roar perhaps alluding to the sound of the door being struck. In Greek mythology, one of Hercules' twelve labours is the slaying of a lion with his bare hands, and one of his attributes is the lion's skin that he wears as a symbol of victory.

The conjunction of Hercules with the lion has long stood as a metaphor for power; the Roman emperor Commodus adopted Hercules' club and pelt as his own attributes and presented himself as an incarnation of the god (Fig. 10). Incorporated into this lyre-shaped doorknocker, the imperial associations of the imagery would have been transferred to the early modern building for which it was made. The precious material of the object, its size, weight, and metaphorical associations, suggest that it functioned not only practically, but in a ritualistic and symbolic capacity. A doorknocker acts as a signal of what lies beyond the threshold; it provides an interface between the everyday world outside and the restricted elevated world within, its Herculean metaphor perhaps suggesting a hereditary right to power. Like the ringing of church bells, the sound of knocking formalises an interaction between outside and inside, at the same time as it emphasises their separation.

Fig. 10 Roman coin; obverse: Commodus wearing lion skin; reverse: Hercules' club in wreath

17
Doorknocker with Hercules and a Pair of Lions
Italy (Venice); *c.*1560–1630
Bronze
35 x 28 x 34 cm
The Fitzwilliam Museum, Cambridge (M.27-1917)

VESSELS AND LAMPS

The vessels, lamps, candlesticks and incense burners displayed here allude to the link between bronze and the creation of spiritual experiences. The generation of light and scent from oil and fire involves a transformation of substances that recalls alchemical processes; the bronze vessel, like the alchemist's crucible, could be seen as a microcosm of the interaction of elements. The Ashmolean incense burner (Cat. 21) was designed to allow smoke to escape from the mouths of the Medusa and the satyr's mask, creating a striking visual spectre through which to evoke a spiritual dimension beyond everyday existence. Lamps and candlesticks (Cat. 23 and 24) imply a similar metaphorical link between the material world and heaven: a claw-footed base, originally cast from life, grounds the object on earth and in nature, while the flame, elevated into the air, signifies a higher spiritual realm. As objects that might reside on a desk, they suggest enlightenment and the contemplation of God through nature.[1] The polymorphic lamp (Cat. 22), which takes a pelican, elephant and satyr for its body, and a wide-open mouth as its aperture, recasts nature as an agent of metamorphosis: it swallows oil and produces light, a process that suggests alchemy and the shape-shifting behaviour of bronze.

Similar functions were already assigned to bronze much earlier, as the antique objects from the Louvre demonstrate (Cat. 18 and 19). While we may not know the specific meanings of their decorations, they are nonetheless highly suggestive of the symbolism invested in bronze as a spiritual medium. The embodiment of Mercury, god of communication, as a perfume burner, or his winged sandal as an oil lamp, reminds us of the close association between gods, planets and metals. The light, smoke and scent meant to emanate from such objects suggest an inner spirit resides within the bronze vessel, which is called forth by fire. The perfume burner shows Mercury with lips of copper and eyes of silver, pure metals that draw our attention to the faculties of verbal and visual communication, while the scented clouds that would have risen from his head hint at a disembodied communication from the gods.

The importance of such objects extended across different cultures, and two Japanese bronzes (Cat. 25 and 26) are included here to allude to universal aspects in the uses and meanings of bronze. Dating to the Meiji period (1868–1912), when Japan was opened to the West, the objects demonstrate the distinctive colouring, style and finish of Japanese bronzes, while their design points to common early traditions. The simple principle of the incense burner, which integrates the object's function with its figurative form, is not dissimilar from antique and Renaissance examples (Cat. 19 and 21). The cockerel, moreover, is a universal solar symbol. Signifying dawn and the cessation of darkness, the cockerel's crowing in Shinto religion is a sacred song that summons Amaterasu, goddess of the sun, while in the New Testament it awakens Peter to his denial and brings enlightenment. Known as an attribute of Apollo and an emblem of Christ, the cockerel's association with the sun, the planetary sign of gold, also figures in alchemy, as an expression of the quest to perfect nature (Fig. 11).

The dragon similarly touches different cultures. Most commonly associated with St Michael's and St George's triumph over evil, dragons are also linked to the generative force of the elements,

Fig. 11 Emblem XXX, 'Luna is as
requisite to Sol as a Hen is to a Cock',
from Michael Maier, *Atalanta Fugiens
hoc est, emblamata nova de secretis naturae
chymica …*, Oppenheim, 1618

residing in water and producing rain. In Far
Eastern iconography, the confrontation of two
dragons embodies a dualism similar to the
caduceus (see Cat. 27 to 31), suggesting a con-
tinual cycle of opposing forces that by turns feed
and neutralise each other. The appearance of
dragons on flower-bowls, such as the one shown
here, hints at the life-giving power of water and
suggests an interplay of elements. Used in the
practice of *Ikebana*, the art of flower arranging,
such objects are distinctively Japanese, yet their
symbolic implications extend beyond the local.
Flowers, like incense, release scent; as expressions
of nature they represent the changing seasons and
the passing of time, fundamental truths that are
affirmed by many of the objects in this room.

NOTE
1 See Thornton, 'The status and display of small bronzes'.

73

18
Oil Lamp in the form of a Sandalled Foot
Byblos, Phoenicia (modern Lebanon);
1st–2nd century AD
Bronze
6.1 x 16.3 x 4.2 cm
Musée du Louvre, Paris (Br 4476)

19
Perfume Vessel: bust of Hermès-Thôt
Lower Egypt; 2nd century AD
Bronze with copper and silver inlay
13 x 10.3 x 6.8 cm
Musée du Louvre, Paris (Br 2940)

20
Aquamanile (Water vessel) in the form of a Lion
Germany (Nuremberg); *c.*1400
Bronze
31 x 33 x 10.6 cm
Rijksmuseum, Amsterdam (R.B.K. 16913)

21
Desiderio da Firenze (attrib.)
(*fl.* 1532–45)
Incense Burner
Italy (Padua); *c.*1530–40
Bronze
Height: 51.3 cm
The Ashmolean Museum
of Art and Archaeology,
Oxford (WA 2004)

22

Grotesque Lamp in the form of an Elephant,
Pelican, Satyr and Mask
Italy (Padua); *c*.1550
Bronze
12 x 20 x 20 cm
The Fitzwilliam Museum, Cambridge (M.8-1965)

23

Workshop of Severo da Ravenna,
Severo di Domenico Calzetto (*fl. c*.1496–*c*.1543)
Oil Lamp formed as a Satyr's Head
on a Claw Foot Stand
Italy (Padua); 16th century
Bronze
20 x 9 x 15 cm
The Fitzwilliam Museum, Cambridge (M.12-1997)

24
Workshop of Severo da Ravenna
Siren Candlestick on a Claw Foot Stand
Italy (Padua); 2nd quarter of the 16th century
Bronze
Height: 28.2 cm
The Ashmolean Museum of Art
and Archaeology, Oxford (WA 1888.CDEF.B1025)

25
Incense Burner in the form of a Cockerel
Japan; c.1800–60
Bronze
36.4 x 27 x 13.1 cm
Victoria and Albert Museum,
London (M1870-1876)

26
Flower Bowl and Stand
Japan; c.1840
Bronze with applied dragon decoration
Bowl Height: 9.4 cm, Diameter: 16.2 cm
Victoria and Albert Museum, London (M1213-1926)

ROOM TWO

POWER AND MORTALITY

INTRODUCTION

The functions and meanings of bronze experienced directly through touch, as in the household or church, are amplified when bronze is used on a larger scale and for public purposes. This room alludes to sculptures that might have been experienced visually, from afar, and which could be ideologically connected with ideas of empire, state and nationhood. Many of these sculptures were made for specific purposes or occasions, for example to convey the legitimacy of a current ruler (Cat. 32) or to commemorate a political episode (Cat. 36). Their meanings are in one sense temporal, in that they can be linked to particular historical moments, but they also transcend their temporality; bronze is prehistoric, and its importance as a medium of power dates back to early forms of government. It asserted the authority of emperors figuratively, in the form of statues and coins, and also didactically, as a carrier of written edicts and laws.

Emperors and kings often portrayed themselves as deities, while their possession of statues of gods hinted at their divine legitimacy. Spanning almost two millennia, the figures of Mercury in this room provide us with a way of visualising the universal importance of allegorical sculpture for disseminating contemporary ideologies. Drawing an uninterrupted lineage from ancient Rome through to the Holy Roman Empire, revolutionary France and modern Germany, the divine messenger Mercury serves as a metaphorical envoy for the higher authorities of government. The constancy of this symbol within these vastly changing political situations ties together the statues and fragments in this room. Whether taking the form

of a symbol or a portrait, all these works essentially function as allegories of their respective political territories; Giambologna's 'Mercury' (Cat. 29), once presented as a gift to Rudolf II, is as potent a symbol of the emperor's rule as the portrait by Adriaen de Vries (Cat. 39).

As the example of Rudolf II illustrates, the imperial ancestry of bronze has been cumulatively absorbed by successive cultures. Modern uses of bronze bear the imprint of antiquity, and the history of ancient empires survives in the relics that continue to form a part of our cities. In Rome, the *Lex de Imperio*, a bronze tablet bearing the decree of the Roman Senate, has remained on view in the Capitoline Museum since its re-discovery in the Renaissance; Paris' Vendôme column, destroyed in the Commune and rebuilt in 1875, deliberately recalls Trajan's column, transferring to Napoleon its ancient imperial lineage (Cat. 35).

Bronze from the past is often handed down to us as remnants, but these broken relics are suggestive not so much of fragility as of endurance and power. Sculptures of any material have always been vulnerable to iconoclasm, but the iconoclasm of bronze is never simply destructive: it is also generative. When bronze is melted down, the form of the object is lost, but the material itself prevails and gives rise to new images. Giambologna's statue of Henry IV (Cat. 34) did not survive the French revolution, but much of its material was reused, creating new icons of the age, and we might imagine Dumont's 'Génie de la Liberté' (Cat. 36) as its symbolic reincarnation.

MERCURY

This process of requisition and appropriation was often orchestrated deliberately as a symbolic index of power. Captured bronze is the victor's trophy, and cannon and statues were melted down and refashioned: the two were literally interchangeable (see Figs 3 and 4). A bronze statue erected in a public square signalled wealth and knowledge, not only by reflecting the ruler's likeness and his purchase of technical ability, but by implicitly demonstrating military prowess and the potential of deciding whether materials and skills were used for sculpture or for war.

In the sixteenth century, it was not unusual to use planets, gods and metals as interchangeable symbols. By name alone, mercury already points to its multiple identities, and its character as a metal is closely linked to its celestial and mythical attributes. Fluid, diffuse and amorphous, mercury defies containment and is difficult to control. Its capricious nature is mirrored in mercury's other incarnations: divine messenger and god of communication, Mercury, with wings at his heels, was also the swiftest planet closest to the sun, symbolising movement and circulation, liveliness, speed and flexibility.

The spiritual and physical attributes of Mercury were of central importance to the work of alchemists and their quest to master the transformation of matter. Mercury acts as the alchemical solvent that can separate and fuse other substances, changing their state and value, while itself remaining passive. One of Mercury's attributes as god of trade is a purse, representing exchange and the alchemical promise of gold; he symbolises not only the alchemist's power to create gold, but ensures its circulation and the expansion of wealth. His image is frequently found on antique coins, like a literal manifestation of his promise (Fig. 1).[1] Mercury's other attribute is the caduceus, etymologically indicating his role as messenger, but also providing a more enigmatic symbol of his character and powers (Fig. 2). The two snakes winding around his staff represent a union of opposites, most commonly known as the apothecary's poison and antidote, but also signalling the alchemist's aspiration to change the states of metals. Mercury's embodiment in bronze could be read as an allegory of the union of copper and tin, female Venus and male Saturn, turning the process of bronze casting into an act of alchemical transmutation and artistic creation.

The examples here, ranging from the second century through to the twentieth, highlight the longevity of Mercury as a symbol. They are at once timeless and of their time; we can recognise even the oldest example, but each figure bears the marks of its age. Only the most ancient (Cat. 27) seems to have been used as a votive statuette; by the time of Giambologna, Mercury functioned as a public emblem. Thought to have been originally commissioned to crown a column at the university at Bologna, Giambologna's flying Mercury was intended to represent the transmission of divine wisdom.[2] Signalling a heightened awareness of the creative possibilities of bronze, the figure became one of the most influential icons of the Renaissance and was widely copied, as this version, thought to date to the early nineteenth century, confirms. Its lasting significance is visible here in François Rude's 'Mercure', and indeed in Augustin Dumont's 'Génie de la Liberté' (Cat. 36); both are distinctly of the nineteenth century, but carry the unmistakable echo of their sixteenth-century forebear. Conversely, the court sculptor Johan Gregor van der Schardt, whose figure was probably made for Emperor Maximilian II, seems deliberately to deny Giambologna's influence. In pose and character, van der Schardt's 'Mercury' is resolutely grounded, not flying, and seems engaged in a conversation, suggesting he is one step ahead: already communicating his message rather than travelling to deliver it. A similar groundedness informs August Gaul's twentieth-century statue. Made as an icon for the Klöpperhaus in Hamburg (originally the offices of wool-trader

Hans Klöpper, and today a department store), it calls on Mercury to ensure wealth and prosperity, suggesting that the talismanic power of the gods remained a potent metaphor into the twentieth century.

NOTES

1 As Pamela Smith shows, the alchemist Joachim Becher used mercurial imagery to contrast his own profession, which created and spread wealth, with that of the treasury official, who was self-interested and discouraged the circulation of money. Smith, *The business of alchemy*, pp. 217–27.

2 Avery, *Giambologna*, pp. 125–7

Fig. 1 Antique coin showing Mercury with caduceus and purse

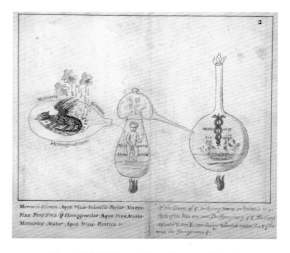

Fig. 2 Rabbi Simon Ben Cantara, 'Our Mercury. The living pontic water', *Cabala mineralis*, first book, folio 2, *c*.1700

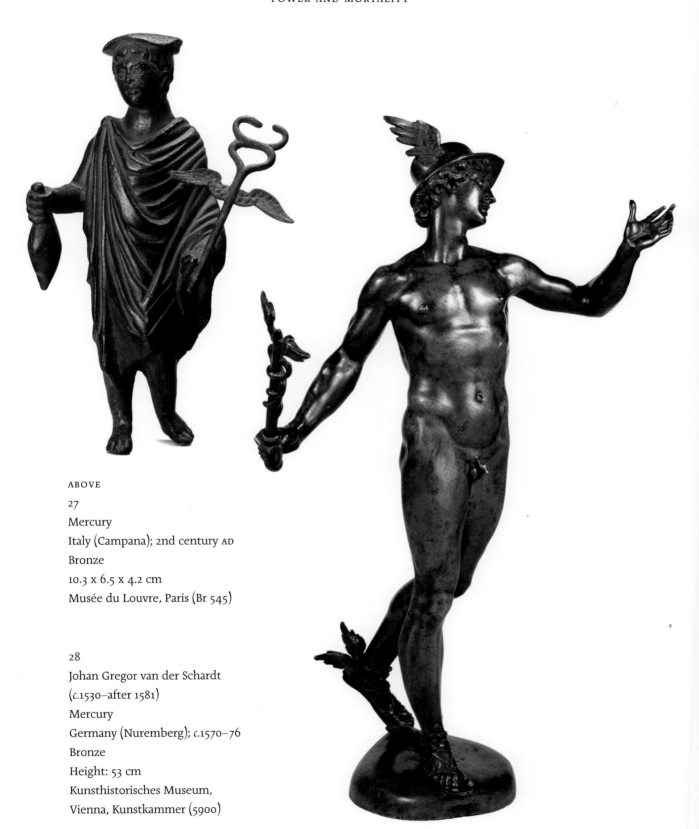

ABOVE

27
Mercury
Italy (Campana); 2nd century AD
Bronze
10.3 x 6.5 x 4.2 cm
Musée du Louvre, Paris (Br 545)

28
Johan Gregor van der Schardt
(c.1530–after 1581)
Mercury
Germany (Nuremberg); c.1570–76
Bronze
Height: 53 cm
Kunsthistorisches Museum,
Vienna, Kunstkammer (5900)

BELOW

29

After Giambologna (1529–1608)

Mercury

Italy (Rome); 1830

Bronze

61 x 13 x 24 cm

The Fitzwilliam Museum, Cambridge (M.3-1854)

ABOVE

30

François Rude (1784–1855)

Mercure rattachant ses talonnières

(Mercury fastening his winged sandals)

France (Paris); cast by F. Barbedienne, 1873

Bronze

109 x 58 x 41 cm

Musée du Louvre, Paris (TH 134)

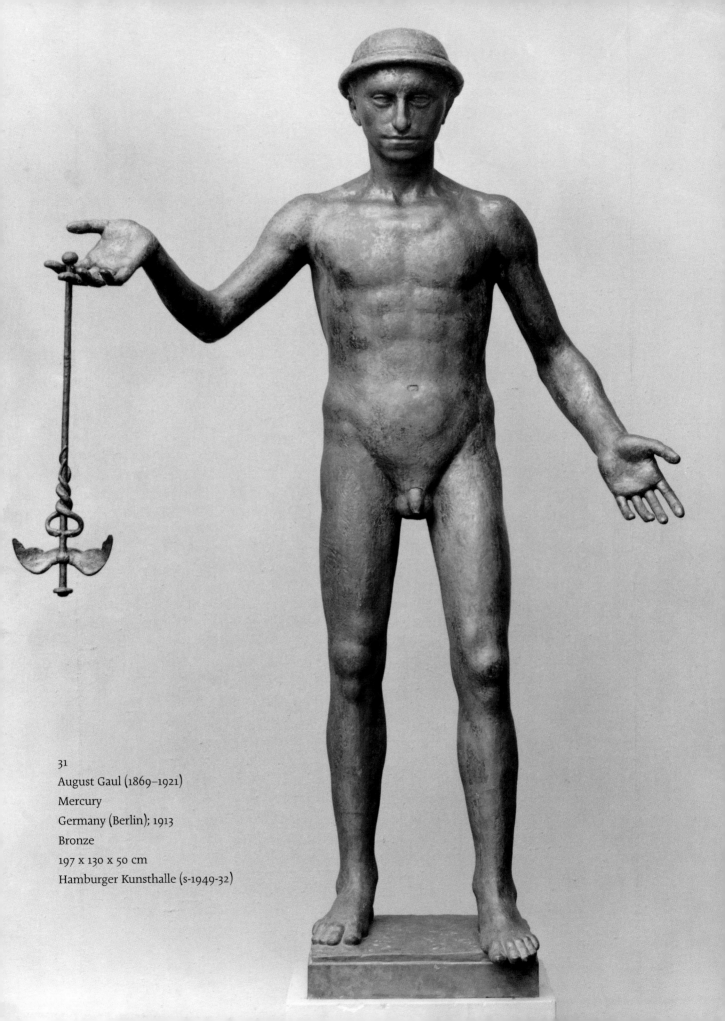

31
August Gaul (1869–1921)
Mercury
Germany (Berlin); 1913
Bronze
197 x 130 x 50 cm
Hamburger Kunsthalle (s-1949-32)

STATUES AND FRAGMENTS

Today we can only imagine the profusion of statues that once stood in imperial Rome. Few survive and most of those, like the head of Roman emperor Hadrian (Cat. 32), as fragments. Other sources enable us to estimate that some four thousand bronze statues, including over twenty equestrian groups, once stood in Rome's open spaces alone, not counting the many others that adorned public buildings, temples and porticoes.[1] Used to depict living and idealised individuals as well as gods, bronze was a powerful device for cultivating fame and reputation.

The link between bronze and power is demonstrated nowhere more visibly than in the monumental equestrian statue, a tradition that over centuries remained inextricably tied to its imperial origin in the statue of Marcus Aurelius. Requiring huge quantities of bronze and superlative casting skills, the equestrian monument was a material symbol of the great investment made in a ruler's image (Figs 3 and 4). Often over life-size in scale and years in the making, it paraded the wealth of an emperor or king, and signalled his access to the science of bronze-casting, a skill useful not only for making statues, but also for manufacturing weapons.

Bronze is associated with permanence and stability, but materially it always embodies change.[2] Equestrian statues are erected to reflect the power of rulers and regimes, but their fate often exposes the temporality of power. The surviving arm of Henry IV's monument (Cat. 34), demolished by decree of the National Assembly on 14 August 1792, shows that the king was dressed in armour, signalling his military prowess and readiness for battle. At the same time, the arm's fragmentary state highlights the flipside of power, in that it indexes another battle, that of the French Revolution, which heralded its own destruction. Other equestrian statues were dismantled during the Revolution, and they were replaced by new emblems that themselves became vulnerable. The horse's head (Cat. 35) was once part of the original reliefs encircling the Vendôme column, cast under Napoleon I from cannon captured at the battle of Austerlitz. The column replaced the equestrian statue of Louis XIV, destroyed in the same year as King Henry's monument.

The impact of the changing political landscape on the production of bronze sculpture can be further traced through Augustin Dumont, whose 'Génie de la Liberté' was commissioned under Louis Philippe's July monarchy, to commemorate the victims of the *Trois Glorieuses* (27, 28 and 29 July 1830). Representing the transition from the old Bourbon monarchy to the constitutional rule of Louis Philippe, the flying figure on the July column marks a key site of the French Revolution, that of the former Bastille prison which became a burial ground for the bodies of the hundreds killed in 1830 and in February 1848. Caught between flight and descent, the poise of the figure echoes the dynamic symbolism of its attributes: the burning torch points to the sky, suggesting enlightenment and the heavenly salvation of the martyrs, while the broken chain is a reminder of the past and suggests that oppression, like iron chains, is man-made and can thus be broken.

The series of changes affecting the Vendôme

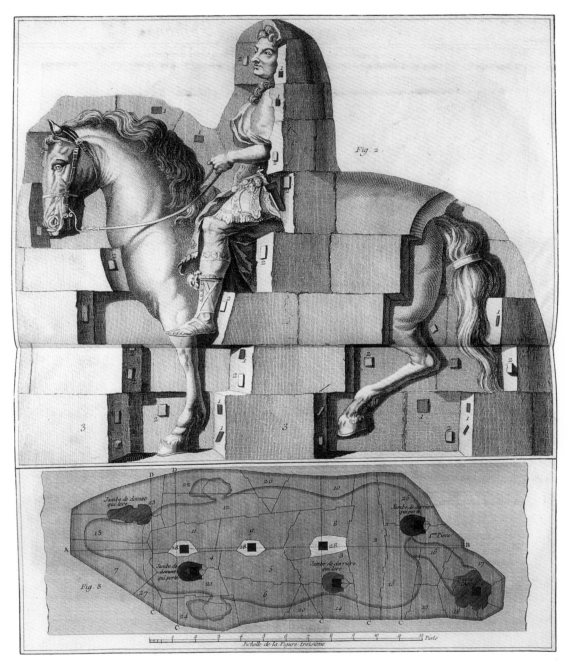

Figs. 3 and 4 Plate 118 and 121 'Casting an Equestrian Statue' from Denis Diderot, *Encyclopédie, ou, dictionnaire raisonné des sciences, des arts et des métiers. Recueil de planches, sur les sciences, les arts libéraux, et les arts méchaniques*, Paris, 1762–72

89

Fig. 4 Plate 121 as overleaf

Fig. 5 Alexandre René Véron
(1826–97), 'Place Vendôme, Paris 1871',
tinted lithograph by Siméon, drawing
by Véron

column are reflected in the mixed fortunes of Dumont's works. The Caesar-like statue of Napoleon I had been removed from the column in 1814, and a succession of emblems replaced it in subsequent years. It was Dumont who created the replica of Napoleon Bonaparte's statue in 1863, under the short-lived regime of Napoleon III. But unlike his 'Génie de la Liberté', which maintained its currency as an emblem, Dumont's Napoleon became a target in the Commune, when the statue and column were razed to the ground, only to be rebuilt in 1875 (see Fig. 5).

The Vendôme column highlights the transient nature of emblematic symbols. A satirical image pointing to Gustave Courbet's involvement in the story of its demolition (Fig. 6) personifies bronze as a medium that expresses the cyclical nature of power. Official guardian of France's artistic treasures during the Commune, Courbet became villainised for his role in the column's fate; the government of the Third Republic sent him to prison for six months and held him liable for the 323,091 francs required for its rebuilding, forcing him into exile.[3] In Bertall's image, bronze statues are stirred to life by the actions of the iconoclast, pleading to be spared from the furnace. It points to the irreverence of Courbet, the modern artist, for symbols of the establishment, but it also implies that bronze communicates with the culture in which it finds itself. We are reminded that iconoclasm can be generative as well as destructive, that renewal and rebirth are only mirrors of devastation and loss, a cycle symbolically embodied in the fluid nature of bronze.

Fig. 6 Bertall, 'Le Citoyen Courbet', *Le Grelot*, Paris, 30 April 1871

NOTES

1 Pliny and Pausanias picture ancient Greek and Roman cities for us, and other evidence is cited in Lahusen, '*Ars Humanissima*' and Mattusch, *Classical bronzes*.

2 The deliberate erasure (or reconfiguring) of the condemned through the removal or destruction of their statues is analysed in Carey, '*In Memoriam*'.
3 Gamboni, *The destruction of art*.

32
The Emperor Hadrian (76–138 AD)
Egypt(?); c.140 AD
Bronze
Height: 43 cm
Musée du Louvre, Paris (Br 4547)

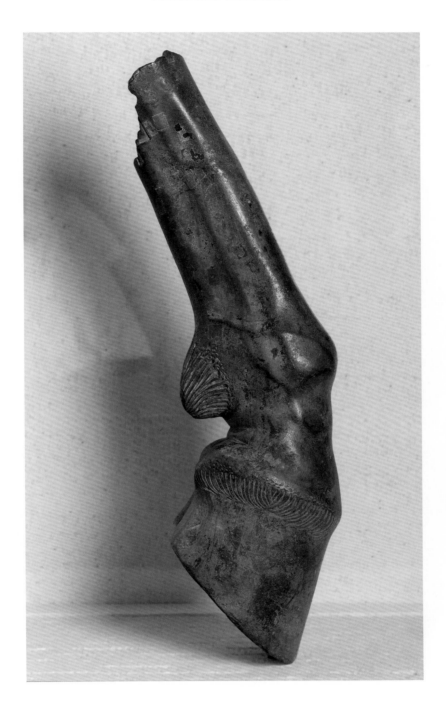

33
Fragment of a Horse's Foreleg
France (near Cassel); Imperial Roman period
Bronze
48 x 11.7 x 13.1 cm
Musée du Louvre, Paris (Br 54)

34
Jean Boulogne (known as Giambologna)
(1529–1608), assisted by
Pietro Tacca (bapt. 1577–1640)
Fragments from the Monument to Henry IV
France (Paris); c.1604–11
Bronze
Left Hand (MR 3453)
31 x 19 x 18 cm
Right Forearm (MR 3450)
80 x 40 x 67
Left Foreleg of Horse (MR 3451)
103 x 26 x 37 cm
All Musée du Louvre, Paris

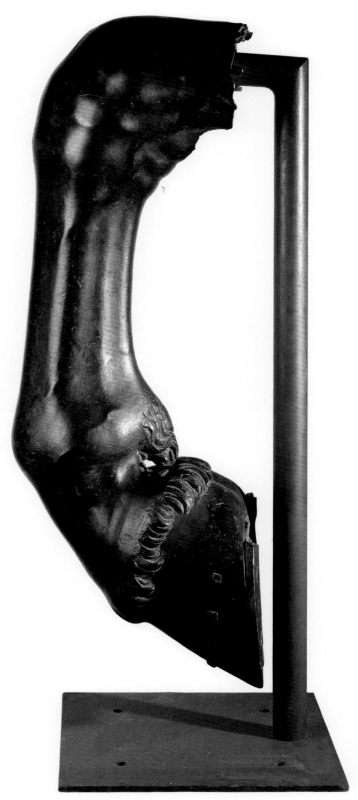

ABOVE

35

Denis Pierre Bergeret (1782–1863)

Fragment of a Horse's Head

Formerly part of the reliefs encircling the

Vendôme column

France (Paris); c.1806–10

Bronze

20.5 x 22.3 x 5 cm

Musée national du château de Compiègne (po 1655)

OPPOSITE

36

Augustin (Auguste Alexandre) Dumont (1801–84)

Le Génie de la Liberté (The Spirit of Liberty)

France (Paris); cast 1885 after the 1833 model for

the July Column, Place de la Bastille, Paris

Bronze

235 x 112 x 130 cm

Musée du Louvre, Paris (RF 680)

ARMOUR

Bronze was the metal of choice for armour before the development of steel, for although much more costly, it was stronger and easier to work than iron. The protective function of bronze armour was symbolically extended by the relief decorations that often adorned its surface. For example, the appearance of Venus on an ancient gladiatorial greave, designed to cover the shin (Cat. 37), can be read as an invocation of divine protection and immortality. Surrounded by a thorny acanthus tree, foretelling the gladiator's suffering, Venus represents his salvation, whether in victory or death. As the planetary symbol of copper, Venus has an additional significance here: she is in attendance not only as an image, but as a material presence, literally shielding the wearer as an embodiment of bronze.

Bronze plates designed to follow the curvature of individual body parts were developed in ancient Greece, and continued to be refined into the modern age. Adriaen de Vries' relief bust of Rudolf II (Cat. 39) shows the emperor wearing a cuirass decorated with emblems of power, including the head of a lion, the figures of Hercules and Minerva, and the golden fleece (the conjunction of Hercules and the lion also appears in the door-knocker, Cat. 17). The heroic and regal demeanour with which the emperor is depicted belies the actual status of his power at this time. Following a revolt in Hungary, most of Rudolf's ruling authority was ceded to his brother Matthias, who took control over Hungary, Austria and Moravia in 1608, a year before de Vries executed the relief. While the portrait can therefore be seen as an attempt to assert the emperor's legitimacy at the court, we could also read it as a signal of the temporality of power. The bronze cuirass suggests an impulse to self-protection; like a talismanic shield, it calls on divine intervention to defend the emperor and guard his material wealth. The prominent visibility of de Vries' name beneath the head of the lion, on the emperor's truncated right arm (Fig. 7), implicates him in his sitter's fate and suggests he wields a power of his own: capable not only of imitating the emperor's likeness to perpetuate his fame, he is also an artificer whose armour can protect and sustain its wearer. As Michael Cole's essay shows (p. 42ff), such portraits may be read as a metaphorical link between the sculptor's profession and that of the armourer.

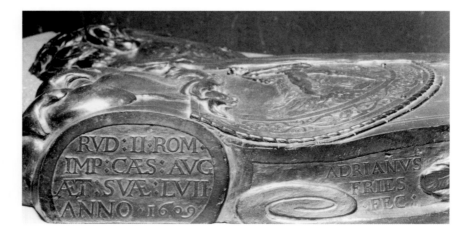

37
Gladiatorial Greave (shin-armour),
decorated with Venus in relief
Roman; 1st century AD
Bronze
28.7 x 15.5 cm
Musée du Louvre, Paris (Br 1143)

38
Gladiatorial Greave (shin-armour)
Italy (Pompeii); 3rd quarter
of 1st century AD
Bronze
57.5 x 17 cm
Musée du Louvre, Paris (Br 1169)

OPPOSITE Fig. 7 Cat. 39 (detail)

ABOVE

39
Adriaen de Vries (c.1545–1626)
Bust in relief, Rudolf II (1552–1612),
Holy Roman Emperor from 1576
Bohemia (Prague); 1609
Bronze
71.5 x 53 cm
Victoria and Albert Museum, London (6920-1860)

OPPOSITE

40
Apollonio di Niccolò Perusini (attrib.) (active 1533)
Culverin (small firearm)
Italy; c.1533
Bronze
10 x 82.5 x 12 cm
The Fitzwilliam Museum, Cambridge (M.4-2003)

CANNON

Cannon embody the ambiguous nature of power. They are used to attack and kill, as well as to defend and protect; they are instruments of war, but silenced cannon also represent peace; they are designed to be destructive, but seized cannon were themselves melted down and refashioned into new objects. Not unlike bells, cannon functioned as much symbolically as practically, and it was partly through sound that their power was asserted.

Some nations, notably Britain, produced very plain cannon, but others invested theirs with astonishing creative programmes, as the Italian 'Furies' cannon demonstrates (Cat. 42). Its striking imagery and craftsmanship transforms, to our eyes, what could have been a perfunctory object into an extraordinary work of sculpture. It seems less surprising, when we look at this object, to learn that the profession of the weapons-maker was often interlinked with that of the sculptor (see Michael Cole's essay).

Perhaps most immediately striking is the contrasts that this cannon sets up: carved wood against cast bronze, the terrible beauty of the carriage against the leafy laurel branches winding around the barrel. The Furies (the Greek *Erinyes*), recognisable by their emaciated bodies, twisted features and flame-like hair, were instruments of divine punishment and vengeance who pursued sinners, symbolically extending the purpose of the cannon they carry. Prophesying damnation and hell, they conjure up the fire of the underworld, an element that is crucial in the operation of cannon. Indeed, the object as a whole could be understood in terms of an interaction of elements. The carriage calls to mind the importance of wood to fuel the furnaces that melt bronze, and fire also ignites the cannon's charge, which flies through air and scorches the earth; as the inscriptions on the barrel state: 'the thunderbolts of earthly war'; 'a single spark suffices'.[1]

NOTE

1 The currency of this notion in the 16th century is suggested in the plate of 'gun powder' in the *Nova Reperta* (see Origins and Properties, p. 61), under which Stradanus wrote: 'Thunder and lightning made by hand. It seems to be a gift from the jealous underworld'. Straet (Stradanus), *Nova Reperta*.

41

Model of a Cannon with the Insignia of Charles IX

France; third quarter 16th century (showing front and back)

Bronze

Length: 44.2 cm

Musée du Louvre, Paris (OA 6946)

42
Alberghetti Foundry
'Furies' Gun
Italy (Venice); 1773
Bronze gun on a wooden carriage
104 x 242 x 117 cm
Royal Armouries Museum of Artillery, Fort Nelson,
Fareham (XIX.79)

42 (detail)
Button at breech end of gun,
with relief of Head of Medusa

ROOM THREE

RETURN TO ORIGINS

INTRODUCTION

The exhibition closes with two works that use bronze in almost opposing ways, one emphasising the material's inherent qualities, the other disguising them. While Mark Manders' piece (Cat. 44) is cast from the artist's handmade model, and painted to look like clay, that of Rudolf Herz (Cat. 43) is cast from a ready-made broom, chemically patinated to resemble weathered bronze. Modelling and shaping clay into figurative images suggests a kind of life-giving process; new forms are brought into being from a mass of clay, itself an organic material. The broom almost implies the opposite, in that it is made by a more formal and impartial process; it takes as its starting point a manufactured, inanimate object, and proceeds to destroy it as it is transformed into bronze.

The visual differences also translate into the metaphorical readings these works offer, with one suggesting a quixotic chain of apparently personal ideas, the other drawing on a manufactured political emblem intended to be publicly understood. Manders presents two animals which are wild, but which interact with our domestic world. Foxes and mice live in holes and burrows; they come out at night and forage in our rubbish. Like intruders, they bring something foreign into our familiar spaces, perhaps the underside of our world or our unconscious. Herz's 'Lenins Besen' (Lenin's Broom) evokes some similar ideas, if with a more calculated symbolism. The broom could be sweeping something under the carpet (the communist era), and burying unwanted thoughts or realities, or it could be sweeping away dust that clouds our thinking, bringing clarity and understanding. In a sense both works embody ideas of concealing and revealing, and this is reflected not only through imagery, but materially, in the way they handle bronze.

Rather than attempting to summarise preoccupations in contemporary sculpture, this last room alludes to some of the connections that current practices have with those represented in older objects in the exhibition. The works shown here inflect the world we know today, but they recall ideas and archetypes that are perpetual. Bronze embodies these continuities, not only because materially and technically it has remained virtually unchanged over hundreds of years, but because it involuntarily brings its own intrinsic properties into whatever context it is used. A broom, or indeed a fox, may be appropriated to service a particular ideology, but in time that ideology will pass; the image, cast into bronze, will still be here and will activate new meanings that reshape our present.

43
Rudolf Herz (b.1954)
Lenins Besen
(Lenin's Broom)
Germany (Munich); 1988
Bronze
220 x 25 x 25 cm
Hamburger Kunsthalle (G-1999-6)

LENINS BESEN

'Lenins Besen' takes an image that was cultivated as a political emblem of Lenin. Even the act of showing such an image today reconstitutes its meaning. The work takes for its source a poster of 1920 by the Russian caricaturist Viktor Deni, in which Lenin is wielding a red broom and sweeping away fat aristocrats, capitalists and clerics from the face of the earth. The broom is a symbol for a new world-order, implicitly purer and more virtuous than the systems of capitalists. Fashioned into a sculpture, the broom becomes like a museum relic from the Lenin-era, yet it materialises what had only ever been a metaphor.

The ordinariness of the broom, and its extraordinary transformation into bronze, plays on the duality of objects that become emblems. Although 'Lenins Besen' points to a highly specific interpretation of Soviet iconography, it also resonates more broadly as a visual index of the temporal and ambiguous nature of emblems. Indeed, we might link the symbolism of the broom to a much earlier source, Hercules cleansing the stables of King Augeas. Diverting a river to help him wash away thirty years of manure from the king's herd of three thousand cattle, Hercules swept the interior of the stables clean; the river, meanwhile, fertilised the barren land outside. Hercules' deed revealed the king's tainted character, which was mirrored not only in the dirty stables but in the deprivation of the fields. The Augean stables, which are still today an idiom for the uncovering of political corruption, suggest that dirt and cleanliness are essentially the same; that dirt is part of the natural order, and only becomes unclean when there is an interference that stops it circulating.

'Lenins Besen' perhaps points to some similar incontrovertible cycles. Lenin swept, but a broom does not erase dirt, it simply redistributes it.
On the one hand, Herz highlights the triviality embodied in politically-charged emblems, but on the other he draws our attention to the symbolic potential of a common household object. Political meanings come and go, but the archetypal meanings they draw on may contain deeper truths that can only be manipulated for a short time.

FOX/MOUSE/BELT

Mark Manders describes his 'Fox/Mouse/Belt' in terms of the possibility of a disappearance. He is fascinated by 'the fact that living creatures can disappear into other creatures, as food, sometimes even when they are still alive': the mouse is strapped to the belly of the fox, but 'could disappear into it later'.[1] We can think of the disappearance of one thing into another as a visual change (if the fox eats the mouse, we no longer see it, but it is still there, inside the fox). But it also suggests a physical change; the mouse could become part of the body of the fox, part of its molecular structure. The sculpture literally exteriorises the cycle of change, and reminds us that bodies have internal spaces that are active and consumptive, not unlike a crucible in which matter is transformed and sublimated.

This idea is also invoked at a material level. The fox and mouse have been modelled and cast into bronze, and then painted to imitate wet clay. While there is no illusion of flesh and fur, there is an illusion of fresh, soft clay, which evokes a sense of the vulnerability of physical things – as though you could hurt the fox by pushing your fingers into the clay, or kill the mouse by squeezing it in your hand and rendering it formless again. For Manders, wet clay is 'the most basic and natural material to use' to make a sculpture, and it suggests that the work has just been made. It is also the first material that is used before a form is cast into bronze, and the two materials therefore have at once an interdependent and mutually exclusive relationship. By making the clay part of the visual experience of bronze, 'Fox/Mouse/Belt' disrupts our expectations of the behaviour of matter.

At more than one level, the work opens up questions about how we perceive and interpret certain physical relationships. The artificial co-existence of clay and bronze is mirrored in the unnatural togetherness of fox and mouse – hunter and prey – entities that normally cancel each other out, but here suggest a kind of inverted birth. The sculpture reminds us that disappearance is itself part of an illusion, and that death is an organic process in which matter is converted, reincorporated and reconstituted into new energy.

NOTE

1 Quotations from *Mark Manders/Singing Sailor*, p. 41.

44
Mark Manders (b.1968)
Fox/Mouse/Belt
Netherlands (Arnhem); 1993
Painted bronze
116.84 x 40.64 x 15.24 cm
Zeno X Gallery, Antwerp

111

Select Bibliography

Publications that pertain to objects in the exhibition are listed alphabetically by the city of lending institutions, followed by a select bibliography relating to notes in the essays and to the themes in the exhibition, divided into primary and secondary sources.

Amsterdam, Rijksmuseum

Kuile, Onno ter, *Koper & brons*, Rijksmuseum, Amsterdam, 1986

Antwerp, Zeno X Gallery

Mark Manders: fragments from self-portrait as a building (exhibition catalogue), Staatliche Kunsthalle Baden-Baden and Douglas Hyde Gallery, Dublin, 1997–8

Mark Manders: parallel occurrence (exhibition catalogue), Irish Museum of Modern Art, Dublin, 2005

Mark Manders/Singing Sailors (exhibition catalogue), Art Gallery of York University, Toronto, 2002

Cambridge, Fitzwilliam Museum

Avery, Charles, *Giambologna: the complete sculpture*, Oxford, 1987

Binnebeke, Emile van, *Bronssculptur: Beeldhouwkunst 1500–1800 in de collectie van het Museum Boymans-van Beuningen. Bronze sculpture: sculpture from 1500–1800 in the collection of the Boymans-van Beuningen Museum*, Museum Boymans van Beuningen, Rotterdam, 1994

Poole, Julia, 'Apollonio di Nicolo Perusin (*fl.*1533), culverin or cannon', in *2003 review: the annual report of the National Art Collections Fund in its centenary year*, 2003, p. 84

Renaissance and Baroque bronzes from the Fitzwilliam Museum, Cambridge (exhibition catalogue), Victoria Avery and Jo Dillon, Daniel Katz, London, 2002

Fareham, Royal Armouries Museum of Artillery, Fort Nelson

Avery, Victoria, 'State and private bronze foundries in Cinquecento Venice: new light on the Alberghetti and di Conti workshops', in Peta Motture, ed., *Large bronzes in the Renaissance*, New Haven, 2003

Blackmore, Howard L., *The armouries of the Tower of London I: ordnance*, London, 1976

Scalini, Mario, *L'arte italiana del bronzo, 1000-1700: toreutica monumentale dall'Alto Medioevo al Barocco*, Busto Arsizio, 1988

Hamburg, Hamburger Kunsthalle

Herz (exhibition catalogue), ed. Peter Friese and Dirk Halfbrodt, Neue Gesellschaft für Bildende Kunst, Berlin, Neues Museum Weserburg, Bremen, and Halle K, Hamburg, 1997

Herz, Rudolf, *Lenins Lager: Entwurf für eine Skulptur in Dresden*, Berlin, 1992

Symaken, Georg, *Die dritte Dimension: Plastiken, Konstruktionen, Objekte. Bestandskatalog der Skulpturenabteilung der Hamburger Kunsthalle*, Hamburg, 1988

Westheim, Paul, 'August Gaul und seine Plastiken am Klöpperhaus in Hamburg', in *Die Kunst*, no. 30, 1914

Kassel, Staatliche Museen

Die Beschwörung des Kosmos: Europäische Bronzen der Renaissance (exhibition catalogue), ed. Christoph Brockhaus, Wilhelm Lehmbruck Museum, Duisberg, 1994

Natur und Antike in der Renaissance (exhibition catalogue), Sibylle Ebert-Schifferer et al., Liebieghaus Museum Alter Plastik, Frankfurt am Main, 1985

Schmidberger, Ekkehard, et al., *Schatzkunst 800 bis 1800: Kunsthandwerk und Plastik der Staatlichen Museen Kassel im Hessischen Landesmuseum Kassel*, Staatliche Museen Kassel, 2001

London, Victoria and Albert Museum

A grand design: the art of the Victoria and Albert Museum (exhibition catalogue), Malcolm Baker and Brenda Richardson, eds, London and New York, 1997

Adriaen de Vries 1556–1626: imperial sculptor (exhibition catalogue), ed. Frits Scholten, Rijksmuseum, Amsterdam, and J. Paul Getty Museum, Los Angeles, 1998

Avery, Charles, 'Guiseppe de Levis (1552–1611/14) and his relatives in the bronze casting industry in Verona', *Estratto da Verona Illustrata*, no. 5, Rivista del Mueso di Castelvecchio, 1992

Earle, Joe, *Flower bronzes of Japan*, London, 1995

Imperial Japan: the art of the Meiji period (1868–1912) (exhibition catalogue), ed. Frederick Baekeland, Herbert F. Johnson Museum of Art, Cornell University, Ithaca, New York, 1980

Larsson, Lars Olaf, *Adrian de Vries*, Vienna and Munich, 1967

Motture, Peta and Stuart Currie, *The sculpted object 1400 to 1700*, London, 1997

Motture, Peta, *Bells & mortars: catalogue of Italian bronzes in the Victoria and Albert Museum*, London, 2001

Munich, Bayerisches Nationalmuseum

Natur und Antike in der Renaissance (exhibition catalogue), Sibylle Ebert-Schifferer et al., Liebieghaus Museum Alter Plastik, Frankfurt am Main, 1985

Weihrauch, Hans R., *Die Bildwerke in Bronze und in anderen Metallen. Mit einem Anhang, die Bronzebildwerke des Residenzmuseums*, Bayerisches Nationalmuseum München, Munich, 1956

Oxford, Ashmolean Museum

Donatello e il suo tempo: il bronzetto a Padova nel Quattrocento e nel Cinquecento (exhibition catalogue), Museo Civico di Padova, Milan, 2001

European bronzes from the Quentin collection: an exhibition at the Frick Collection (exhibition catalogue), Manfred Leithe-Jasper and Patricia Wengraf, New York and Milan, 2004

Penny, Nicholas, *Catalogue of European sculpture in the Ashmolean Museum 1540 to the present day*, 3 vols, Ashmolean Museum, Oxford, 1992

Verber, Monique, 'Desiderio da Firenze's bronzen parfumbrander', *Bulletin van het Rijksmuseum*, vol. 51, no. 1, 2003, pp. 6–27

Warren, Jeremy, *Catalogue of European sculpture in the Ashmolean Museum, mainly pre-1540*, Oxford, forthcoming

Warren, Jeremy, *Renaissance master bronzes from the Ashmolean Museum, Oxford: the Fortnum Collection* (exhibition catalogue), Daniel Katz and the Ashmolean Museum in association with the National Art Collections Fund, Oxford, 1999

Paris, Musée du Louvre

Avery, Charles, *Giambologna: the complete sculpture*, Oxford, 1987

Baratte, Sophie, ed., *Les bronzes de la couronne*, Musée du Louvre, Réunion des musées nationaux, Paris, 1999

Calmette, Joseph, *François Rude*, Paris, 1920

Daniel Katz: European sculpture (exhibition catalogue), Johannes Auersperg and Katherine Zock, Daniel Katz, London, 2000

Demange, Françoise and Alain Erlande Brandenburg, 'Une réduction de canon à l'emblématique de Catherine de Médicis', *Revue du Louvre*, 1980, 2, pp. 109–14

Descamps-Lequime, Sophie, et al., *Les antiquités grecques du Louvre*, Musée du Louvre, Réunion des musées nationaux, Paris, 2002

Pasquier, Alain, *The Louvre: Greek, Etruscan, and Roman antiques*, trans. Kenneth Painter, Musée du Louvre, Paris, 1991

Lemaistre, Isabelle Leroy-Jay, et al., *Sculpture française, II: Renaissance et temps modernes*, Musée du Louvre, Réunion des musées nationaux, Paris, 1998

Vienna, Kunsthistorisches Museum

Leithe-Jasper, Manfred, *Renaissance master bronzes from the collection of the Kunsthistorisches Museum Vienna*, Kunsthistorisches Museum, Vienna, 1986

Lichtenberg, H. Honnens de, *Johan Gregor van der Schardt, Bildhauer bei Kaiser Maximilian II., am dänischen Hof und bei Tycho Brahe*, trans. Georg Albrecht Mai, Copenhagen, 1991

Natur und Antike in der Renaissance (exhibition catalogue), Sibylle Ebert-Schifferer et al., Liebieghaus Museum Alter Plastik, Frankfurt am Main, 1985

Pechstein, Klaus, ed., *Bronzen und Plaketten vom ausgehenden 15. Jahrhundert bis zur Mitte des 17. Jahrhunderts*, Kunstgewerbemuseum Berlin, Staatliche Museen Preussischer Kulturbesitz, 1968

Prag um 1600: Kunst und Kultur am Hofe Kaiser Rudolfs II (exhibition catalogue), Villa Hügel, Essen, and Kunsthistorisches Museum, Vienna, 1988

Further reading

Primary sources

Agricola, Georgius, *De re metallica* (Latin, Basel, 1556), first full English trans. Herbert Clark Hoover and Lou Henry Hoover (1912), London, 1950

Barnaud, Nicolas Delphinas, *The book of Lambspring: concerning the philosophical stone* (Latin, Frankfurt, 1599), in *The Hermetic Museum restored and enlarged*, trans. Arthur Edward Waite, London, 1893

Biringuccio, Vannoccio, *The pirotechnia, treatise on metals and metallurgy* (Italian, Venice, 1540), first English trans. Cyril Stanley Smith and Martha T. Gnudi (1942), London, 1996

Boffrand, Germain, *Description de ce qui a été pratiquée pour fondre en bronze d'un seul jet la figure equestre de Louis XIV: elevée par la ville de Paris dans la place de Louis le Grand, en mil six cens quatre-vingt-dix-neuf*, Paris, 1743

Cellini, Benvenuto, *The life of Benvenuto Cellini* (Italian, Florence, begun *c.*1562, published 1728), first English trans. Thomas Nugent, London, 1771 (also trans. John Addington Symonds, London, 1888, 1995)

Cellini, *The treatises of Benvenuto Cellini on goldsmithing and sculpture* (Italian, Florence, 1568), first full English trans. Charles Robert Ashbee, London, 1898

Cocteau, Jean, *La mort et les statues*, photographs by Pierre Jahan, Paris, 1946

Diderot, Denis, *Encyclopédie, ou, dictionnaire raisonné des sciences, des arts, et des métiers*, par une société de gens de lettres, 17 vols, Paris, 1751–65 (sections later republished as *Diderot pictorial encyclopedia of trades and industry*, New York, 1959)

Ercker, Lazarus, *Treatise on ores and assaying* (German, Prague, 1574), first English trans. Sir John Pettus, London, 1683 (also trans. Anneliese Grünhaldt Sisco and Cyril Stanley Smith, Chicago, 1951)

Falconet, Etienne Maurice, *Pieces written by M Falconet and M Diderot on sculpture in general, and particularly on the statue of Peter the Great*, trans. W. Tooke, London, 1777

Ferber, Johann Jacob, *Beyträge zu der Mineralgeschichte von Böhmen*, Berlin, 1774

Gaffurio, Franchino, *The theory of music* (Latin, Milan, 1492), ed. Claude V. Palisca, trans. Walter Kurt Kreyszig, New Haven, 1993

Gowland, William, *The art of casting bronze in Japan: a paper read before the Applied Art section of the Society of Arts on April 23rd, 1895*, London, 1895

Havard, Henry, *Les bronzes d'art et d'ameublement*, Paris, no date, before 1900

Kalbe, Ulrich Rülein von (attrib.), *Bergwerk und Probierbüchlein. A translation from the German of the Bergbüchlein, a sixteenth-century book on mining geology* (German, Augsburg?, 1500), trans. Anneliese Grünhaldt Sisco and Cyril Stanley Smith, New York, 1949

Maier, Michael, *Atalanta Fugiens* (Latin, Oppenheim, 1617), trans. and ed. H.M.E. de Jong, *Michael Maier's Atalanta Fugiens, sources of an alchemical book of emblems*, Leiden, 1969

Mariette, Pierre Jean, *Description des travaux qui ont précédé, accompagné et suivi la fonte en bronze d'un seul jet de la statue équestre de Louis XV le bien-aimé, dressée sur les mémoires de M. Lempereur, ancien echevin*, Paris, 1768

Montfaucon, Bernard de, *L'antiquité expliquée et représenté en figures*, 10 vols, Paris, 1719

Pausanias, *Description of Greece*, trans. Peter Levi, 2 vols, 1971

Pliny, *Natural history, Books XXXIII–XXXIV*, trans. H. Rackham, Cambridge, Mass. and London 1995

Straet, Jan van der (also known as Johann Stradanus), *Nova reperta: the sciences, inventions and discoveries of the middle ages and the renaissance as represented in 24 engravings issued in the early 1580s* (Latin, Antwerp, c.1600), ed. Bern Dibner, Norwalk, Conn., 1953

Theophilus, Presbyter, *On divers arts* (Germany, Latin, c.1125), trans. John G. Hawthorne and Cyril Stanley Smith, Chicago and London, 1963

Varchi, Benedetto, *Questione sull'alchimia*, Florence, 1827

Vasari, Giorgio, *Vasari on technique* (Florence, Italian, 1550), trans. Louisa S. Maclehose, ed. George Baldwin Brown, New York, 1907

Secondary sources

À fleur de peau: le moulage sur nature au XIXe siècle (exhibition catalogue), ed. Edouard Papet, Musée d'Orsay, Paris, 2002

Ahl, Diane Cole, ed., *Leonardo da Vinci's Sforza monument horse: the art and the engineering*, London and Bethlehem, 1995

Amico, Leonard N., *Bernard Palissy: in search of earthly paradise*, Paris, 1996

Baker, Malcolm, *Figured in marble: the making and viewing of eighteenth-century sculpture*, Los Angeles and London, 2000

Bandman, Günther, 'Bemerkungen zu einer Ikonologie des Materials', *Staedel Jahrbuch*, no. 2, 1969, pp. 75–100

Beer, Carel de, *The art of gunfounding: the casting of bronze cannon in the late eighteenth century*, Rotherfield, England, 1991

Beke, Làszló, 'The demolition of Stalin's statue in Budapest', in *L'art et les révolutions* (Section 4, les iconoclasms), ed. Sergiusz Michalski, Strasbourg, 1992, pp. 275–83

Butters, Suzanne B., *The triumph of Vulcan: sculptors' tools, porphyry, and the prince in ducal Florence*, 2 vols, Florence, 1996

Carey, Sorcha, 'In Memoriam (Perpetuam) Neronis: "Damnatio Memoriae" and Nero's Colossus', *Apollo*, vol. 152, no. 451, July 2000, pp. 20–31

Cole, Michael, *Cellini and the principles of sculpture*, Cambridge, 2002

Craddock, Paul T. and Alessandra R. Giumlia-Mair, *Corinthium Aes: das scharze Gold der Alchimisten*, Mainz am Rhein, 1993

Eliade, Mircea, *The forge and the crucible*, trans. Stephen Corrin, London, 1962

Fabrique d'art: la Compagnie des Bronzes, 1854–1979 (exhibition catalogue), ed. Guy Lemaire, La Fonderie, Brussels, 2003

Farago, Claire, ed., *Reframing the Renaissance: visual culture in Europe and Latin America 1450–1650*, New Haven and London, 1995

Fontijn, David R., *Sacrificial landscapes: cultural biographies of persons, objects and 'natural' places in the Bronze Age of the Southern Netherlands, c.2300–600 BC*, Leiden, 2003

Forbes, Robert James, *Metallurgy in antiquity: a notebook for archaeologists and technologists*, Leiden, 1950

Gamboni, Dario, *The destruction of art: iconoclasm and vandalism since the French Revolution*, New Haven and London, 1997

Gramaccini, Norberto, 'Zur Ikonologie der Bronze im Mittelaltar', *Staedel-Jahrbuch*, New Series, no. 11, 1987, pp. 147–70

Haskell, Francis, and Nicholas Penny, *Taste and the antique: the lure of classical sculpture 1500–1900*, New Haven and London, 1981

Hayward, John, *Virtuoso goldsmiths and the triumph of Mannerism 1540–1620*, London, 1976

Kellenbenz, Hermann and Jürgen Schneider, eds, *Precious metals in the age of expansion*, Stuttgart, 1981

Kellenbenz, Hermann, ed., *Schwerpunkte der Kupferproduktion und des Kupferhandels in Europa 1500–1650*, Vienna, 1977

Kris, Ernst, 'Der Stil "Rustique": Die Verwendung des Naturabgusses bei Wenzel Jamnitzer und Bernard Palissy', *Jahrbuch der Kunsthistorischen Sammlungen in Wien*, New Series, no. 1, 1928

Lahusen, Götz, '*Ars Humanissima:* zur Ikonologie des Materials der Römischen Plastik und Skulptur', in *Acta Hyperborea*, no. 4, Cophenhagen, 1992, pp. 173–95

Lahusen, Götz, *Römische Bildnisse aus Bronze: Kunst und Technik*, Munich, 2001

Matthew, Leslie G., *Antiques of the pharmacy*, London, 1971

Mattusch, Carol C., *Classical bronzes: the ancient craft of Greek and Roman statuary*, Ithaca and London, 1996

Michalski, Sergiusz, 'Die Pariser Denkmäler der III. Republik und die Surrealisten', in *Idee, Werke, Theorien, Dokumente, Jahrbuch der Hamburger Kunsthalle*, no. 7, 1988, pp. 91–107

Montagu, Jennifer, *Gold, silver and bronze: metal sculpture of the Roman Baroque*, Princeton, 1996

Montagu, Jennifer, *Roman Baroque sculpture: the industry of art*, New Haven and London, 1989

Morel, Philippe, *Les grottes maniéristes en Italie au XVIe siècle: thèâtre et alchemie de la nature*, Paris, Macula, 1998

Motture, Peta, ed., *Large bronzes in the Renaissance*, New Haven, 2003

Newman, William, *Promethean ambitions: alchemy and the quest to perfect nature*, Chicago, 2004

Penny, Nicholas, 'Non-finito in Italian fifteenth-century bronze sculpture', in *La scultura, antologia di belle arti*, no. 48–51, 1994, pp. 11–15

Penny, Nicholas, *The materials of sculpture*, New Haven and London, 1993

Pincus, Debra, ed., *Small bronzes in the Renaissance*, New Haven, 2001

Raff, Thomas, *Die Sprache der Materialien: Anleitung zu einer Ikonologie der Werkstoffe*, Munich, 1994

Ruhm und Sinnlichkeit, Innsbrucker Bronzeguss 1500–1650 (exhibition catalogue), Tiroler Landesmuseum Ferdinandeum, Innsbruck, 1996

Schenker, Alexander M., *The bronze horseman: Falconet's monument to Peter the Great*, New Haven and London, 2004

Second skin: historical life casting and contemporary sculpture (exhibition catalogue), ed. Stephen Feeke, Henry Moore Institute, Leeds, 2002

Smith, Pamela H., *The body of the artisan: art and experience in the scientific revolution*, Chicago, 2004

Smith, Pamela H., *The business of alchemy: science and culture in the Holy Roman Empire*, Princeton, 1994

Stone, Richard E., 'Antico and the development of bronze casting in Italy at the end of the quattrocento', *Metropolitan Museum Journal*, no. 16, 1981, pp. 87–116

Summers, David, *The sculpture of Vincenzo Danti: a study in the influence of Michelangelo and the ideals of the Maniera*, New York, 1979

Tarkovski, Andrei Arsenévich, et al., *Andrei Rublev* (Russia, 1966), film, distributed New York, Fox Lorber Home Video, 1992

The fire of Hephaistos: large classical bronzes from North American collections (exhibition catalogue), ed. Carol Mattusch, Harvard University Art Museums, Cambridge, Mass., 1996

Thornton, Dora, 'The status and display of small bronzes in the Italian Renaissance interior', *The Sculpture Journal*, no. 5, 2001, pp. 33–41

Von allen Seiten schön, Bronzen der Renaissance und des Barock: Katalog zur Ausstellung der Skulpturensammlung der Staatlichen Museen zu Berlin, Preussischer Kulturbesitz im Alten Museum (exhibition catalogue), ed. Volker Krahn, Heidelberg, 1995

Wagner, Monika, *Das Material der Kunst: eine andere Geschichte der Moderne*, Munich, 2001

Wagner, Monika, Dietmar Rübel, Sebastian Hackenschmidt, *Lexikon des künstlerischen Materials: Werkstoffe der modernen Kunst von Abfall bis Zinn*, Munich, 2002

Wenzel Jamnitzer und die Nürnberger Goldschmiedkunst 1500–1700 (exhibition catalogue), ed. Gerhard Bott, Germanisches Nationalmuseum Nürnberg, 1985

Wrigley, Richard, 'Breaking the code: interpreting French Revolutionary iconoclasm', in Alison Yarrington and Kelvin Everest, eds, *Reflections of revolution: images of Romanticism*, London, 1993

Acknowledgements

Sabine Conrad, Richard Clay (University of Birmingham), Sophie Descamps (Musée du Louvre), Gabi Dolff-Bonekämper (BDA Landesverband, Berlin), Nathalie Dupuis (Musée des arts decoratifs, Paris), Rudolf Herz, Claudia Kryza-Gersch (Kunsthistorisches Museum, Vienna), Greg Irvine (V&A), Andrew Lacey (Alchemy Sculpture Studio), Isabelle Leroy-Jay Lemaistre (Musée du Louvre), Philip Magrath (Royal Armouries, Leeds), Philippe Malgouyres (Musée du Louvre), Ewa Manikowska (National Museum of Warsaw), Laure de Margerie (Musée d'Orsay, Paris), Nicholas Mead, Sergiusz Michalski (Eberhard-Karls-Universität, Tübingen), Peta Motture (V&A), Angus Patterson (V&A), Julia Poole (Fitzwilliam Museum), Lynne Richards, Frits Scholten (Rijksmuseum, Amsterdam), Bryan Sitch (Hull & East Riding Museum), Jeremy Warren (Wallace Collection), Timothy Wilson (Ashmolean Museum)

Photographic credits

Introduction

Fig. 1 Conway Library, Courtauld Institute of Art
Fig. 2 EPA/Alberto Martin

Bronze, the Mythology of a Metal

Fig. 1 Courtesy Mosfilm Studio, Moscow
Fig. 2 © 2000, Photo Scala, Florence
Fig. 3 © Rijksmuseum, Amsterdam
Fig. 4 Courtesy Ignazio Vok
Fig. 5 © Bayerisches Nationalmuseum, Munich
Fig. 6 SMK Foto
Fig. 7 © Photo CNAC/MNAM Dist. RMN/© Philippe Migeat/© Mimmo Paladino

Under the Sign of the Vulcan

Fig. 1 © Alinari/Art Resource, NY
Fig. 2, 17 Scala/Art Resource, NY
Fig. 3 Courtesy Laboratorio Fotográfico de la Biblioteca Nacional, Madrid
Fig. 4 Courtesy Germanisches Nationalmuseum, Nuremberg
Fig. 5 © Bayerisches Nationalmuseum, Munich
Fig. 6, 7, 9, 10 © KHM, Wien
Fig. 8 © 1990, Photo Scala, Florence, courtesy of the Ministero Beni e Att. Culturali
Fig. 11 © Museo Nacional del Prado
Fig. 12 Courtesy Bayerische Staatsgemäldesammlungen, Munich
Fig. 13, 15 The author
Fig. 14 © Staatliche Museen Kassel, photo: Ute Brunzel
Fig. 16 © Patrimonio Nacional

Origins and Properties

Fig. 1 and p. 53 The Royal Collection © HM Queen Elizabeth II
Fig. 2 Librairie Charles Delagrave, Paris
Fig. 3, 11 Courtesy Glasgow University Library, Dept. of Special Collections

Fig. 4 © KHM Wien
Fig. 5, 6 © Collections artistiques de l'Université de Liège
Fig. 7 © Leiden University Library
Fig. 8 © Photo RMN © Hervé Lewandowski
Fig. 9 © The Trustees of the British Museum/© 2005 House of Commons Library
Fig. 10 Courtesy Classical Numismatic Group Inc.

Cat. 1, 7, 20 © Rijksmuseum, Amsterdam
Cat. 2, 3, 4, 9, 10, 25, 26 V&A Images/Victoria and Albert Museum
Cat. 5, 12, 13 © KHM, Wien
Cat. 6 Leeds Museums & Galleries, Temple Newsam House
Cat. 8, 17, 22, 23 © Fitzwilliam Museum, University of Cambridge
Cat. 11, 14 © Staatliche Museen Kassel, Photo: Ute Brunzel
Cat. 15 © Bayerisches Nationalmuseum, Munich
Cat. 16 © Photo RMN/© Les frères Chuzeville
Cat. 18, 19 © Photo RMN/© Hervé Lewandowski
Cat. 21, 24 Ashmolean Museum, University of Oxford

Power and Mortality

Fig. 1 Courtesy dirtyoldcoins.com, photo: Rasiel Suarez
Fig. 2 © The British Library
Fig. 3, 4 © 2004 Smithsonian Institution
Fig. 5 Brown University Library
Fig. 6 Reproduced with permission of the University of Sussex
Fig. 7 V&A Images/Victoria and Albert Museum

Cat. 27, 33, 36 © Photo RMN/© Hervé Lewandowski
Cat. 28 and p. 81 © KHM, Wien
Cat. 29 © Fitzwilliam Museum, University of Cambridge
Cat. 30, 41 © Photo RMN © Jean-Gilles Berizzi
Cat. 31 © Hamburger Kunsthalle/bpk, photo: Elke Walford
Cat. 32 © Photo RMN/© Patrick Leroy
Cat. 34 © PMVP/Photo: Degraces/Briant Remi
Cat. 35 © Photo RMN © Franck Raux
Cat. 37, 38 © Photo RMN/© Gérard Blot
Cat. 39 V&A Images/Victoria and Albert Museum
Cat. 40 © Fitzwilliam Museum, University of Cambridge
Cat. 42 © Board of Trustees of the Armouries

Return to Origins

Cat. 43 and p. 105 © Hans Döring, Munich/© DACS 2005
Cat. 44 Courtesy Zeno X Gallery, Antwerp, Photo: Dirk Pauwels

Published to accompany the exhibition
Bronze: the power of life and death

Henry Moore Institute, Leeds,
15 September 2005 – 7 January 2006

The Henry Moore Institute
is part of The Henry Moore Foundation

Curated by *Martina Droth*

Exhibition display coordinated by *Stephen Feeke*

Catalogue prepared and published in Great Britain
by the Henry Moore Institute, 74 The Headrow, Leeds, LS1 3AH

Catalogue edited by *Martina Droth* and *Penelope Curtis*
Catalogue coordinated by *Gill Armstrong*
Picture research by *Gill Armstrong*

ISBN 1 900081 74 1

Designed by Raymond Carpenter
Typeset by Tom Knott
Printed by Specialblue

FRONT COVER
Cat. 27, 'Mercury', Musée du Louvre, Paris
© RMN/© Hervé Lewandowski

BACK COVER
Cat. 31, 'Mercury', Hamburger Kunsthalle
© Hamburger Kunsthalle/bpk, photo: Elke Walford